THE TRIAL

Jean-Louis Barrault and André Gide

André Gide & Jean-Louis Barrault

THE TRIAL

A Dramatization Based on Franz Kafka's Novel

Translated by Leon Katz

SCHOCKEN BOOKS • NEW YORK

Translated from LE PROCÈS (Pièce tirée du roman
de Kafka) par André Gide et Jean-Louis Barrault
© Editions Gallimard 1947

PREFATORY NOTE
by André Gide

I am anxious, first, to make one point clear: without Jean-Louis Barrault, this play inspired by Kafka's celebrated novel would not be in existence—nor would my translation of *Hamlet,* whose great success stems from his performance. Our meeting in Marseilles is recorded in my *Journal.* It was on May 4th, 1942. I was on the verge of leaving the following day for Tunis, where I was forced to remain during the whole of the oppressive German occupation. Jean-Louis Barrault and Madeleine Renaud invited me to lunch; an excellent meal, of which I have the most pleasant recollection, and during which the great actor urged me to complete the translation of *Hamlet.* I had finished the first act twenty years before. His urging was so friendly and eloquent that I took up this commission almost as soon as I arrived in Tunis, and did not leave off until I had finished it.

On that same day, Jean-Louis Barrault also spoke to me of his plan to stage Kafka's *The Trial,* and asked if I would agree to help him. I had the greatest admiration for this strange work, but told him that before deciding I would have to reread it. Which I did. I must admit that at first the difficulties facing such an adaptation seemed insurmountable to me. But that was to underestimate the genius of Jean-Louis Barrault. When I came back to France in '45, he returned to the attack. He had worked on his own, had already prepared in detail a sort of scenario which he submitted to me. A great deal more aware than I of the resources and possibilities of the stage, he faced the most formidable difficulties with a courage, and intrepidity that I alone would not have hazarded at all, but which, sustained by him, I undertook wholeheartedly. There was no more to do than to flesh out the skeleton he had brought me. I did everything required immediately, fascinated, delighted, and I gave myself to the work happily, eagerly, enthusiastically. For the rest, I could avail myself frequently of the text of Vialatte's excellent (French) translation. Rarely did I add to the "heart of the work," suppressing my own voice entirely in deference to Kafka, all of whose intentions I was anxious to respect. If this effort bears the success I believe it merits (for I consider it most remarkable, in its form, in its presentation, in its range), it is above all to Jean-Louis Barrault, as originator and creator as well as interpreter, that the credit should redound.

December, 1946

CHARACTERS
in order of appearance

Part One

JOSEPH K., MANAGER OF A BANK

FRANZ, 1ST GUARD

WILHELM, 2ND GUARD

MRS. GRUBACH, LANDLADY

INSPECTOR

THREE BANK EMPLOYEES

DEPUTY DIRECTOR OF THE BANK

MISS BURSTNER

TORTURER

CHILDREN

LAUNDRESS

STUDENT

BAILIFF

ACCUSED MEN

SECOND BAILIFF

YOUNG GIRL

ELEGANT GENTLEMAN

Part Two

FEMALE EMPLOYEE

VARIOUS BANK CLERKS

UNCLE

LENI

ADVOCATE HULD

CHIEF CLERK OF THE COURT

BLOCK, A MERCHANT

THE GREAT JUDGE

MESSENGER

IMPORTANT CLIENT

THREE ANNOYED CLIENTS

LITTLE GIRLS

TITORELLI

JUDGE

CHAPLAIN

INSPECTOR

TWO GUARDS

LADY

GENTLEMAN

FIRST PART

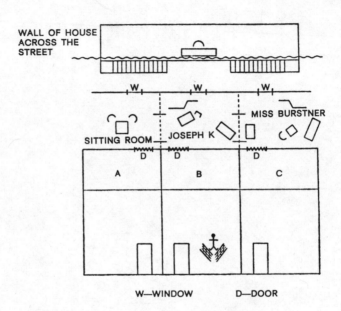

WALL OF HOUSE
ACROSS THE
STREET

W—WINDOW   D—DOOR

SCENE ONE

The stage is divided into three parts; a curtain opens on the central part B: Joseph K's room.
Joseph K has just finished shaving. He dries his razor, sings, combs his hair, tears a page from the calendar hanging on the wall and reads:

K

"Peace on earth to men of good will."
(Then, somewhat mockingly, throwing the crumpled sheet away:)
A-men!
(He puts his shoes on; then suddenly notices the date on the calendar.)
Damn! Today is my birthday! . . . Forgot it completely. I'll bet if my nice little neighbor Miss Burstner knew it, she'd bring me a bunch of violets . . . a modest one, like her income . . . What should I do for my birthday? . . . Something special . . . something I don't do every day. I'm sick of what I do every day.
(Having washed and dressed, but still in his shirtsleeves, he goes up to the table where he expects to find his breakfast.)
My breakfast! . . . What's happened to it? . . . Where is it? . . . Oh, that Mrs. Grubach! She's forgotten to bring it! . . .

Now she'll make me late!
(He rings.
In the window of the house opposite, the face of an old
woman appears. She is looking into K's window. K shrugs
his shoulders, puts on his collar and cufflinks.)
I wonder what got into her this morning? Imagine Mrs.
Grubach forgetting about me!
(He rings again.)
Really, she's never done this before.
(He goes to the hall door, and in passing the window, he
sticks out his tongue at the woman in the window, who
disappears at once. He calls.)
Mrs. Grubach! . . . Mrs. Gru . . .
(The door on the A side of the stage opens slowly. The
First Guard, Franz, appears.)
What do you want?

FRANZ

You rang.

K

I rang for the maid.

FRANZ

Why?

K

What do you mean why?

FRANZ

I'm asking you why you rang for the maid.

K

Why? To have her bring my breakfast.

FRANZ

His breakfast!
(He laughs gently.
He comes into the room, and closing the door slowly, he
addresses someone else who is not seen.)

FRANZ

He claims he rang for the maid to bring his breakfast!
(Low laughter is heard from the next room.

The curtain of wall A rises and reveals the Second Guard
seated between the window and the table leafing through
a book.

K

Now, look, I don't claim anything.
(Then, almost furiously:)
And what are you doing here, in my room?

FRANZ

Easy! Easy! Now you've got to understand that . . .

K

No, I don't. I don't have to understand anything, and what's
more I don't want to. Why the devil did Mrs. Grubach let
you in? I'm going . . .
(The First Guard has come into K's room and is looking
around. K goes into the other room.)

SECOND GUARD

(Without budging)
You can't leave this room.

K

All right, that's enough of this. Just exactly who are you?

SECOND GUARD

None of your business.
(He rises.)
We've come to arrest you.

K

Arrest me! . . . Why?

SECOND GUARD

It's not our job to tell you why. Go into your room and wait.
That's the best thing you can do.

FRANZ

Remember we're being very nice to you. We have nothing
against you personally. If all your guards from now on are
as nice to you as we are, you'll have no reason to complain.
*(Both walk about and inspect: Franz in K's room, and the
Second Guard in Part A, which is the sitting room.)*

K

Guards! What do you mean?

SECOND GUARD

There are charges against you. You'll find out all about it
soon enough.
(Franz examines K's nightshirt.)

FRANZ

You always find out soon enough.
(He examines K's linen with the air of a connoisseur.)
Don't you have anything not so fancy? Why don't you let us
look after your things . . . Because at the depot . . .
(He gathers it all together carefully.)
at the depot, you never know what will happen. The guards

6

sell everything and if the case drags on for long, they forget to keep accounts.

(He puts down the pile of linen in the sitting room. He glances at the Second Guard. He turns again to K.)

The nicest way to do it is to let us take charge of all of it right away. Do you see what I mean?

K

No, but it strikes me . . . Yes, of course! You gentlemen were looking for somebody else and came here by mistake. Or is it some of my friends at the bank playing a practical joke . . . maybe for my thirtieth birthday?

(He laughs in a forced way.)

All right, now tell me . . . The joke was fine, but it's gone far enough.

(The two guards study him coldly.
Mrs. Grubach enters with the tray.)

MRS. GRUBACH

(Seeing the guards)
Oh, excuse me . . .
(She turns to leave.)

K

Come in, Mrs. Grubach.

SECOND GUARD
She can't come in.

K
Why not?

SECOND GUARD
Because you're under arrest.

K

How can I be under arrest?

FRANZ

(Being the good fellow)

Come on! Are you starting that all over again?

(To Mrs. Grubach, who has stopped at the door.)

Give me the tray.

(To K)

You'd better go into your room.

*(K returns to his room and looks nervously for his identi-
fication papers. Meanwhile the two guards sit down to K's
breakfast. K comes back.)*

K

Here are my papers. Please look at them. You'll see from
them that you've made a mistake.

*(The two guards stop for a moment, look at K, look at each
other, and then go on eating.)*

Now show me your warrant for my arrest.

FRANZ

(His nose in his cup)

God-oh-God, how stubborn can you be?

SECOND GUARD

Why do you want to irritate us?

(Very calmly, cutting his bread)

Don't you see that right now we're the best friends you have
in the world?

K

Naturally.

FRANZ

But it's true.

(The two guards eat and drink wolfishly. They cut slices of bread, and spread them with butter and honey.)

K

Here are my papers.

SECOND GUARD

What should we do with them?

FRANZ

You're acting like a child.

SECOND GUARD

(Who goes on eating)

Can't you get it through your head that it makes no difference to us who you are? We're only a couple of guards. We take our orders from the lowest ranks. But before we're sent out, the authorities know to a button the reasons for an arrest. As it happens, your case isn't just a little misdemeanor, as they say. According to the Law, it's one of those cases that are started automatically by the crime itself. When one like yours comes up, the authorities themselves have to conform to Higher Regulations. That's the Law. There can't be any mistake about that.

(The last two sentences and the two preceding words are uttered very precisely. The rest, mumbled, very rapidly, with mouth full, and almost unintelligibly. After they have stuffed themselves full, they use toothpicks for some time.)

K

I don't know this Law.

9

FRANZ

You hear that? He doesn't know the Law.

SECOND GUARD

(Slowly)

Then how can you know you're not guilty?

FRANZ

It's incredible! There's no way to make him understand.

K

I'll clear this up with your superior. I want to see him.

FRANZ

You'll see him when he sends for you. That's not for you to
decide. Now take my advice and go back to your room.
(K complies.)

SECOND GUARD

(Speaking out of the room to the other.)
Try to rest now; build up your strength; you'll need it.

*(K in his room looks for a chair; he settles for the edge of
the bed.*
*Franz, who has risen, looks through the room; he finds a
pack of cigarettes, lights one and puts the pack into one of
his many pockets.)*

FRANZ

If you have any money, maybe we could get some breakfast
for you in the café around the corner.

*(In the window across the street, the old woman, still
curious, has brought an old man to look with her.)*

(K has found an apple on his night table, and munches on it.)

K

Damned fools! They'll make me late for the bank. . . . What can I tell the Manager? I'll tell him . . . the truth.
(He sits.)
He'll never believe it. Of course, I have witnesses.
(He looks at the old people.)
If those two don't want to be dragged into this as witnesses, they'd better stop staring at me.
(He gets up.)
I don't care who stares at me; I have nothing to hide from anybody.
(He goes to his wardrobe.)
And I don't give a damn about their breakfast; where's my bottle?
(He takes a drink; then he pours another glass which he raises to his lips, when from the wings, a tremendous voice is heard:)

VOICE

JOSEPH K . . .

K

(Astonished, stops his movement.)

VOICE

The Inspector wants you.

K

At last!
(He drinks the second glass, then goes to the door. The guards stop him.)

FRANZ

Do you want the Inspector to see you dressed like that? Have you no decency?

K

(Stepping back)
When you drag a man out of bed in the morning do you expect to find him dressed in evening clothes?

FRANZ

Never mind what we expect. You have to be properly dressed.

K

(Putting out a grey jacket on a chair)
Is this proper enough, this coat?

SECOND GUARD

No, it has to be black.
(Franz removes his tie, gently.)

FRANZ

And no loud ties.
(K puts on a dress-coat. He is ready. The two guards tap him on the shoulder.)

SECOND GUARD

You can be very nice, when you aren't making a fuss.

FRANZ

You see, we can get on real well together. Wilhelm, tell the Inspector he's ready.
(Wilhelm, the Second Guard, leaves, picking up the pile of linen on the way. K follows him; Franz, at his heels, stuffs into his pocket one of the shirts that fell down.)

12

Curtain C goes up, and the third room is seen: Miss Burst-
ner's room. There is a folding screen, rug, photographs. A
night table stands in the center of the room. The Inspector,
seated in profile to the audience, fingering the objects on
the night table: a candle, a matchbox, a sewing-kit and a
pin-cushion. There is a chest in the room. Three young
men are there, uninterested observers. The Inspector has
placed his bowler hat on the bed. A white blouse is hanging
from the window latch. The two guards sit down mechani-
cally on the chest. The three gentlemen show no reaction.
K walks in on this scene. Taken aback, he hesitates for an
instant as he enters. From the house across the street, the
old woman, the old man and a large man with a pointed
reddish beard and in a rumpled shirt are watching the
spectacle of the guards and K. The Inspector studies K and
riffs through the slips of paper he has pulled out of his
pocket like a deck of cards.

INSPECTOR

Joseph K . . .
(K, disturbed by the oddity of the situation, bows hesi-
tantly.)
You were surprised by this morning's visit, eh?

K

(Suddenly very friendly)
Oh well, Inspector, I didn't expect it, of course. But I'm
really not too surprised.

INSPECTOR

Ah! You say not *too* surprised.

K

Well, I mean . . . Let me explain . . . May I sit down?

INSPECTOR

It's not customary.

K

You'll understand, I'm sure. I've been on my own in the world ever since I was a boy. I was an orphan, and my uncle brought me up. Well, since things haven't always been easy, I've become more or less immune, so to speak . . . more or less immune to surprises. I don't take them so tragically any more—especially not this one.

INSPECTOR

And why especially not this one?

K

Well, I mean . . . not tragically, but just the same seriously. I'm overlooking, of course, the idea that it's just a practical joke. I thought at first . . . but . . .
(The cold look of the Inspector puts him off. The Inspector counts over the matches in one of the boxes and says:)

INSPECTOR

Quite so.

K

But it's been no use going over my conduct in the past—I can't find a thing to reproach myself with. You'll excuse me if I don't come to all this very . . . if I look at the whole business *(He hesitates.)* as not too serious.

INSPECTOR

You're wrong.

(During this whole scene the Inspector does not stop play-

*ing with the objects within reach, particularly with the
matches he has taken out of the box, and with which he
amuses himself by arranging them on the table in geo-
metrical patterns. He looks up at K only rarely. The two
guards and the three young men remain indifferent.)*

K

Well, all that's neither here nor there. What matters most to
me is: who accuses me. You see, I'm not asking any more what
I'm accused of—but who thinks I've done it. *(K is troubled
by the Inspector's silence.)* In other words, what authority
directs this trial. If I knew, maybe I could . . . Listen:
you, all of you, are acting under somebody's orders. Whose?
I take it for granted you're officials of some kind. But since
you're not in uniform, it seems likely that . . . Well, among
gentlemen, there shouldn't be any trouble coming to an
understanding. I think a little frank, polite explanation will
clear up the whole mess. Then we can shake hands amiably,
you can leave, and we'll all be friends.

INSPECTOR

(Who finally turns to him)
Listen to me, my amiable friend: you're making a great mistake. These gentlemen and myself have been sent here as
part of the trial preliminaries . . . Let me repeat: *trial preliminaries.* And in them, we have a very secondary function,
not to say a downright subordinate one. We hardly know
anything about your case, who accuses you or what of. As a
matter of fact, you're not just accused, you're arrested, which
isn't quite the same thing . . . that's the story, that's the fact.
Whatever the guards could tell you over and above that is
just so much talk. But it's not my job to answer your questions, it's yours to answer mine. And when you're questioned
—not before. Now since you seem to be a fairly decent fellow

15

(He rises to walk toward K.) I'll give you some advice: don't spend so much time figuring us out, and think a little more about yourself. And then don't make such a to-do about your innocence. That spoils the rather good impression you make otherwise. You talk too much. It's what you do that matters.

K

(With apparent composure)
All right then. The State's Attorney, Mr. Hasterer, is a good friend of mine. I want to call him.

INSPECTOR
Go ahead . . . But there's no point in it.

K

No point! And what you're doing here, is there any point in that? You suddenly pounce on me, pin me down, snort over everything I say, analyze everything I do; and when I want to phone the State's Attorney, the one friend I have who might know something about this, to tell him I'm under arrest, to ask him what in God's name it means, you have the cheek to tell me there's no point in it . . .

INSPECTOR
Forgive me.

K
All right, I won't call.

INSPECTOR
No, no, call him by all means.

K
No, I don't want to any more.
    (He goes to the window sulking. He sees the three nosey

16

people at the window across the street.)
Go away!
*(They disappear. K turns to the Inspector, and in a con-
ciliatory, almost jocular tone, says:)*
Gentlemen, you've convinced me. You've done beautifully.
The first act of your little comedy couldn't have been better.
I'm impressed. Now whatever else happens, please don't
think before you go—I'm afraid you must be going now—that
we can't shake hands when we say goodbye.
*(He puts out his hand to the Inspector, who looks at it,
takes his bowler hat from Miss Burstner's bed and adjusts
it before the mirror.)*

INSPECTOR

It isn't as simple as you'd like it to be, or as you try to make
out. But actually there's no reason to despair. The plain
fact of the matter is, you're under arrest. There's nothing
more just now. I came only to tell you so, and to see how
you would take it. That's enough for today. Now you can
go on to your bank, as I think you were planning to do, and
go about your business as usual.

K

To the bank! I thought I was under arrest!

INSPECTOR

You are, but one thing doesn't interfere with the other.
You can do what you were doing as if nothing happened,
at least as far as anyone knows. But only for now, that goes
without saying. So they won't notice at the bank, even though
you'll be late, I had these three men who work with you
brought here. They'll go back with you, and you can explain
you've been out with them on business.
(The two guards disappear.)

K

How do you do? I'm sorry I didn't recognize you before.
(*The three employees, insignificant underlings, bow cere-*
moniously with silly smiles on their faces. K shakes hands
with them and leaves escorted by them.)

Change of scene, underscored by a lighting change and
the accompaniment of street noises and monotonously
repetitive music.
Mrs. Grubach's furtive appearance gives away the fact
that she has been listening at the door. The drop showing
the house across the street disappears. A platform is seen
which rises 6½ feet above the ground, on which K's office
at the bank is located. To right and left of the platform
are flights of steps leading up to K's office.
Downstage, there is a street where busy pedestrians are
hurrying by. The bank's employees go up and down the
platform steps. Others are swallowed up into a vaulted
passage cut through the middle of the platform under
K's office. K, flanked by the three employees, emerges from
the tunnel and climbs the steps with them. Clients press
around him, try to get into his office, but are held back
by subordinates. K sits before his desk.
Orchestration of bank noises: typewriters and ringing tele-
phones. A secretary gives K letters to sign. A group of
bank employees, mostly women, making up a sort of dele-
gation before which the clients and the subordinates step
aside, bring a modest bouquet of flowers to K for his birth-
day. Suddenly one ring drowns out all the others. Every-
one freezes and all other sounds stop. K lifts the receiver
from one of his two office telephones [there is one on his
right and another on his left] and without putting it to
his ear, holds it in the air and waits. Out of the silence
comes the voice from a loudspeaker.

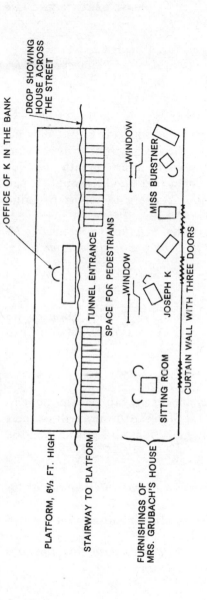

PLATFORM, 6½ FT. HIGH

OFFICE OF K IN THE BANK

DROP SHOWING HOUSE ACROSS THE STREET

STAIRWAY TO PLATFORM

TUNNEL ENTRANCE

SPACE FOR PEDESTRIANS

WINDOW

WINDOW

MISS BURSTNER

JOSEPH K

SITTING ROOM

FURNISHINGS OF MRS. GRUBACH'S HOUSE

CURTAIN WALL WITH THREE DOORS

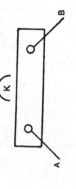

A   K   B

THE LOUDSPEAKER

May I speak to the Manager, Mr. Joseph K?

(In pantomime—a smile of acquiescence, movement of K's lips in an assent that is not heard.)

THE LOUDSPEAKER *(continues)*

Forgive me for disturbing you at your work. But it is important that you know this: the investigation is proceeding normally. Since we are anxious to interfere with your job as little as possible, we thought that Sunday would be particularly convenient for you. You are to report to Julius Street, at the house of . . . .

(The voice breaks off abruptly. K holds the receiver to his ear in vain, shakes it. The bank's activities resume.)

K

Fine! We're cut off!

(As he puts down the receiver, the Deputy Director, for whom everyone makes way, approaches K, smiling and obsequious.)

DEPUTY DIRECTOR

K, I'm having a little party aboard my sailboat this Sunday. Will you come? Hasterer, the State's Attorney, will be there . . . I think he's a friend of yours. Is it all right for Sunday?

K

(Obviously upset and annoyed by the interruption of the telephone call.)

Please excuse me, Mr. Director. But I'm afraid that this particular Sunday, I won't be free.

(Another ring on the phone. The Deputy Director takes up the phone and says, slightly annoyed:)

DEPUTY DIRECTOR

That's all right, I won't insist.
*(He puts the receiver to his ear and immediately hands
the phone to K, saying:)*
I think this is for you.
*(He leaves at once.
The same silence and immobility as during the first tele-
phone call. The same attitude assumed by K.)*

LOUDSPEAKER

We will do our best to make it pleasant for you, and interfere with your job as little as possible.
*(K answers into the receiver. His lips move, but the words
are inaudible.)*

LOUDSPEAKER

We'll make it for Sunday then. You are to appear at 14
Julius Street.
(K's answer is not heard.)
No. No trouble at all. We're entirely at your service. All you
have to do is ask for Lanz the carpenter.
(Same business for K)
Yes, simply say: Carpenter Lanz.
*(K puts down the receiver. He looks suddenly very tired,
done in. He looks at his watch. All the noises and activities
resume. But a prolonged whistle indicates the end of the
work-day. All the employees quit work. The light dims
gradually, and the curtain slowly falls.)*

END OF SCENE ONE

SCENE TWO

The wall-curtain comes down and the three-part division of the first scene is again shown.

    A—Mrs. Grubach's room.

    B—Joseph K's room.

    C—Miss Burstner's room.

It is night, and the wall of the house across the street is not seen. Moonlight falls on the bed in Miss Burstner's room.

When curtain A rises, Mrs. Grubach is sitting before her table, which is lighted by a lamp, busy mending socks. K appears downstage, from the left, moving slowly, looking anxious and despondent. He passes door A, turns to door B (his room), changes his mind and returns to door A. He knocks on it. Then curtain A rises.

K

Still working, Mrs. Grubach?

MRS. GRUBACH

(Continues her mending.)

Oh, there's a lot to do. All day long, my time belongs to my lodgers. At night I do a little work for myself. It's the only time left for me.

23

K

I came to apologize for the bother you had this morning.

MRS. GRUBACH

For what? Oh, you mean those gentlemen who called . . .
I've tidied everything up again.

K

You know, of course, that I had nothing to do with it.

MRS. GRUBACH

That's just what I supposed.
(K has sat down opposite her, a bit embarrassed. Silence.)

K

And it won't happen again.

MRS. GRUBACH

(After a pause, during which she threads her needle.)
That's just what I said to myself.

K

(Upset)
What was that?

MRS. GRUBACH

(Smiling)
Well . . . that it could hardly happen again.
*(She takes her scissors, snips a thread, and goes back to
her work.)*

K

You really think it won't?

24

MRS. GRUBACH

Oh, you mustn't take it so much to heart. You see a lot of that sort of thing in a lifetime . . . Since you're being so frank with me, I may as well tell you I eavesdropped a tiny bit behind the door. And those two guards told me a few things too. I know you've been arrested, but not the way a thief is arrested. If you're arrested as a thief, now that . . . that, they said, is a bad business. But this arrest of yours . . . well, there's something almost learned about it. Excuse me if I talk foolishly.

K

But it isn't foolish at all, Mrs. Grubach.

MRS. GRUBACH

(Encouraged)
Something learned that no one really understands.

K

I'd even go further, Mrs. Grubach. I didn't want to mention it to you, but I did want the opinion of a sensible person, and I'm very glad we see it the same way.

MRS. GRUBACH

After all, isn't it true, that we don't always have to understand?

K

Well, I apologize for the disturbance.

MRS. GRUBACH

Not at all, not at all.

K

Since you don't hold it against me, let's shake hands.
*(Mrs. Grubach puts down the stockings she was darning,
but instead of taking K's hand, she picks up another stock-
ing and K finishes his ineffectual gesture by scratching his
nose. Mrs. Grubach continues in a somewhat different
tone:)*

MRS. GRUBACH

You see, all I want is to keep my house respectable . . . And
things like this are no help.

K

*(Already much affected by the way in which Mrs. Grubach
got out of taking his hand, rises brusquely.)*
I understand, Mrs. Grubach . . . I'm prepared to give notice.

MRS. GRUBACH

(Suddenly compassionate and almost tender)
Oh, don't misunderstand what I said.
*(K is, at the moment, upset. He prepares to leave. At the
door, he says:)*

K

Is Miss Burstner in?

MRS. GRUBACH

(Smiling)
She's still at her theater. She doesn't get back until quite
late. *(She looks at K intently.)* Would you like me to take
a message to her?

K

(Confused, looking down)

Oh! I only wanted to apologize to her for breaking in to
her room this morning.

MRS. GRUBACH

It won't make any difference to her. Anyhow, I put everything back in place already. Would you like to see?
(She is about to get up.)

K

I believe you, Mrs. Grubach.

MRS. GRUBACH

(Rethreading a needle)
It really shouldn't bother you. People of her sort aren't very
tidy anyway. *(She is about to cut a thread.)* She does, on
occasion, you know, receive in her room . . . almost anyone . . .
(Mrs. Grubach is stopped by K's sudden outburst.)

K

That's absolutely not true. *(Trying to calm down.)* Let me
contradict you, Mrs. Grubach, as strongly as I know how.
I've known Miss Burstner for a long time, and I . . .

MRS. GRUBACH

(Brushing away a few ready tears)
Oh please, please, I didn't mean to offend you . . .

K

(Embarrassed)
I'm sorry, Mrs. Grubach. You know I get upset and right
away my nose starts to itch and I want to fight. *(He tries to
laugh.)* Well, good night, Mrs. Grubach.

27

(He leaves.)

(While he is going out to his room)

MRS. GRUBACH

(Sententiously)
He makes me laugh with his nose *(She clips a thread.)* and
his itching. *(She looks for her needle.)* People like him . . .
They call them something . . . what's that word for them?
(Again threading a needle.) Some . . .
   *(Curtain B rises, showing K's room. He has come in. Here
   begins a double scene, in which the speeches of K and
   Mrs. Grubach alternate. The monologue of each is broken
   by the speeches of the other. K performs absurd calis-
   thenics, his legs in the air.)*

K

When we can do what we want to do, that's when we're free.
   (Mrs. Grubach continues her darning.)

MRS. GRUBACH

My lodgers are free to do whatever comes into their heads.

K

(Seated)
Now if I'm free, then I'm not under arrest.

MRS. GRUBACH

But some of them abuse their privilege. And then the others
get annoyed.

K

(Dejected)
I feel I'm free, but I know I'm under arrest.
   (He gets up, sighing.)   ·

MRS. GRUBACH

(Sighing also)
Just the same, they don't arrest you for nothing.

K

(Lights a cigar, and his puffs punctuate his words.)
In my case, it can't be anything so learned as she says. It's really the craziest nonsense!

MRS. GRUBACH

(Working)
But it's silly to take it so seriously.

K

I shouldn't let myself be upset.

MRS. GRUBACH

They get arrested and they don't know why.

K

But it's a surprise, all right. And then you're so little pre-pared. First thing in the morning. *(Very fast.)* At the bank I'd have known what to say, how to answer them. I have a private secretary, just for me, a telephone for local calls and another one for long distance. There are always clients, people coming and going; but no matter how busy I am I always have my wits about me.

MRS. GRUBACH

(Almost dovetailing with K's monologue:)
Me, I'm only a plain landlady. And when they're nice to me . . . Well, I listen a little bit behind doors, but just to keep things from getting out of hand. And then, those guards, I got a little out of them, without letting on . . .

29

K

(Putting out his cigar)
Nothing ought to have happened, nothing.

MRS. GRUBACH

They said—you understand, of course, we have our orders.

K

(Thinking he heard some steps on the staircase, hurries out to the hall, then comes back and sits on his bed.)
They're only the subordinates. What I have to find out is who gave them their orders.

MRS. GRUBACH

(Puts away her sewing and gets ready to leave.)
Oh, but he isn't a bad sort, really. Just a little headstrong. *(She gets up, picks up the basketful of stockings and the lamp just before leaving.)* Ah, I've got it now! The word is— impetuous!

K

(Seated)
The main thing is to keep calm. Keep the situation under control. *(He stretches out on his bed.)*

(Eleven o'clock strikes. Footsteps are heard going up two flights of stairs. K sits up in bed. The sound of the steps comes nearer. He gets up, goes to listen in the corner of the hall vestibule.
Miss Burstner appears downstage left and comes forward, tired, and moving listlessly. As she reaches her room [C], K, in a hushed tone:)

K

Miss Burstncr!

MISS BURSTNER

Who is it?

K

It's me, Joseph K. . . . Next door.

MISS BURSTNER

Oh, it's you . . . Good evening, Mr. K.
  (They shake hands.)

K

There's something I have to tell you.

MISS BURSTNER

Right now?

K

I've been waiting for you for over an hour.

MISS BURSTNER

Couldn't you have told me this morning!

K

It didn't happen until today.

MISS BURSTNER

It's just that I'm very tired. But if it won't take too long . . .
Could you come in for a moment . . . We can't talk here
without waking everyone up . . . Put out the light in the
hall when I put mine on.
  *(K, on tiptoe, goes to put out the light in his room and
  waits in the hall.)*

MISS BURSTNER

Well, are you coming? *(He does.)* Sit down . . . All right,
I'm listening.

K

Oh, I know very well you'll say that it wasn't so urgent, and
that I should have . . .

MISS BURSTNER

Please get to the point. I hate prefaces and introd . . .

K

(Cuts into her sentence to finish the word:)
-ductions. I wanted to apologize to you if you found your
room upset.

MISS BURSTNER

But it's not upset at all.

K

Yes, I was afraid that . . . because this morning, some people
let themselves in here . . . It wasn't my fault.

MISS BURSTNER

Then why are you apologizing?

K

It wasn't exactly my fault, but it happened because of me.

MISS BURSTNER

You're being very confusing. What are you talking about?
(She looks around the room.) Oh, yes, my pictures are out
of place. Then there were people here. Why did they come

in? I hate people coming in while I'm away. You shouldn't
have . . .

K

I can't tell you how sorry I am, and I've been wanting to
apologize to you all day. I would never take it on myself to
touch anything in your room, and certainly not those pictures. Family pictures, I suppose?

MISS BURSTNER

No. But that's hardly the point.

K

I suppose it isn't. They were ignorant boors, three bank
clerks the examining officer brought with him. I'll have
them fired.

MISS BURSTNER

The examining officer!

K

Oh, not for you! What I've been getting at is that this morning they came to arrest me.

MISS BURSTNER

(With sudden interest)
No! Hurry up and tell me, what for?

K

That's exactly what I've been asking myself. You don't have
much experience in matters of law, do you?

MISS BURSTNER

No, but I find legal knots very exciting. The law is wonder-

fully seductive, don't you think so? I'll know a lot more
about it in a few days. I'm taking a job in a law office.

K

Then maybe you can be of use to me in my trial.

MISS BURSTNER

Why not? I love to be of use.

K

You see, the whole business is too unimportant to bring to
a lawyer. But I could certainly do with some advice.

MISS BURSTNER

Well then, first you'll have to tell me what it's about.

K

Yes, of course, but the odd thing is, I don't know myself.

MISS BURSTNER

Listen, Mr. K. If you're making fun of me, you could have
chosen a better time. I told you I'm awfully tired.
*(She stretches out on her bed as if to bring their conver-
sation to a close.)*

K

I'm sorry, but I wasn't joking. I'm afraid it will all turn out
to be more serious than I thought. I mentioned an examining commission, but only because I don't know what else
to call it. In fact, there was no interrogation or investigation
of any kind. I simply was arrested . . . by a whole delegation.

MISS BURSTNER
(Laughing)
Tell me, what was it like?

34

K

(Disturbed by the seductive pose that she has fallen into, and as though losing the thread of his thought)
Horrible.

MISS BURSTNER

That's not specific enough.

K

(After a short pause, snaps back vigorously:)
You want particulars? Can I move the night table?

MISS BURSTNER

What for?
(Sullen before because she was tired, Miss Burstner enters into the game, more and more amused. K begins a burlesque pantomime à la Charlie Chaplin.)

K

To show you exactly how those clowns behaved, it's most important. Me, I'm the Inspector. Over there, the two guards are sitting on the chest. And the three bank clerks are standing in front of the pictures. On the window latch, a white blouse . . . I mention it only to help me remember. And now it begins. Ah! I almost forgot the most important character: myself.
(Suddenly serious, stops play-acting.)
You don't know me, Miss Burstner. I might strike you as awkward and cowardly—this morning's business shattered my nerves. But once I'm up in arms, watch out! I'm not afraid of anything. And I can fight. No one is going to walk over me.
(He returns to his miming.)
I was standing here, across from the night table. The In-

spector was sitting very comfortably, legs crossed . . . a perfect
boor. I must tell you first that the two guards the minute
they came into my room began to help themselves to all
my linen.

MISS BURSTNER

(More and more interested, fascinated by K's pantomime.
At these last words, she gives vent to her indignation.)
Oh!

K

(Continues)
—to all my linen. But that's just incidental. The Inspector
yelled out my name as if he were waking me from the dead.
It was a regular trumpet call. To show you what it was like,
I'll have to yell too.
(Miss Burstner laughs a great deal during his whole pan-
tomime. She tries with a gesture to stop K from shouting,
but she is too late.)

K

(At the top of his voice:)
JOSEPH K . . .
(Immediately, a tattoo of knocks is heard, rapped on the
wall near Miss Burstner. She puts her hand to her heart,
feeling suddenly ill. K, startled, rushes to her.)
Don't be frightened! I'll take care of it.

MISS BURSTNER

(Whispering rapidly:)
It's Mrs. Grubach's nephew, . . . The police captain. He
sleeps on that side. I forgot all about him. Why did you
have to shout? I understood well enough. Go on! Get out!
Now he's listening at the door. He's heard everything. Oh,
my God, what a mess!

K

Come over here . . . He won't be able to hear us . . .
(She goes to him and lets herself fall into his arms.)

MISS BURSTNER

Now, go, go quickly . . . Hurry up and go!

K

You're not angry with me?

MISS BURSTNER
(Letting herself be covered with kisses)
No, I'm never angry with anyone.

*(Before he goes, he kisses her face and neck greedily and
passionately . . . K returns to his room and stretches out on
the bed . . Miss Burstner puts the night table back in its
place, puts out the light, undresses behind the screen.
Moonlight floods her room; she moves through it, a
shadowy figure, and gets into bed.)*

K
(Lying down)
Can anyone feel free? . . . Believe that he's free and know that
he's under arrest?
*(He speaks with more and more confusion, his vague efforts
at thought like those of someone falling asleep. Sound
effects, indicating the breathing of Miss Burstner and K,
and of the regular beating of their hearts.)*
It's just a matter of reparation . . . preparation . . . to head
off the accusation . . . the important thing is: vindication . . .
declaration . . . in preparation . . . ration . . .
(Meanwhile the heartbeats grow faster. K moves restlessly

in his bed. Sighs are heard; they get louder, become real
cries.)

Intense, weird lighting on a strange scene: The two guards
who at the beginning of the play came to arrest K are cow-
ering before a torturer, dressed in a sort of medieval cos-
tume, who towers over them.

TORTURER

Take off your coats and strip to the waist.
(Their moanings stop. Only the beating, which has become
irregular, continues.)

K

(Half-dressed on his bed)
What are you doing there?

FIRST GUARD (FRANZ)

We're going to be flogged because you denounced us.

SECOND GUARD (WILHELM)

You said we took your linen.

FRANZ

Of course we shouldn't have, but if you only knew how little
they pay us! Your fine linen was such a temptation!

WILHELM

It can't be of any use to you any more, since you're under
arrest. I have a family to feed and Franz wanted to get
married. We try to get along as well as we can.

BOTH TOGETHER

Why did you denounce us?

K

(As if in a dream)
I didn't ask them to punish you!

FRANZ

It's just as I told you, Wilhelm. You see, this gentleman didn't even know we would be punished.

K

I only told Miss Burstner!

WILHELM

The Law knew it. And now we're done for. Our career is ruined and now we have to take a horrible beating.

TORTURER

That's enough talk. Get ready. *(To K, who has sat up in bed.)* You mustn't believe everything they say. Fear of the beating is driving them crazy. *(To Franz and Wilhelm:)* All right, strip.

K

(Cries out)
Stop! I'll pay you anything you want if you let them go.

TORTURER

You can't bribe me. I'm an employee of the Court myself. It pays me to whip them, and I'll whip.

(Cries of the two guards. The random noises begin again. The beating grows wilder. K jumps out of bed. The vision disappears at once. The noises grow weaker. Nothing remains but the pulsation which gets more and more regular. Three o'clock strikes. K goes back to bed.)

K

(To himself)
Mustn't take all that too seriously.
(The breathing sounds continue.)
But just the same, must try to get it cleared up.
(Five o'clock strikes. Breathing sounds go on.)
Carpenter Lanz.

Dawn.
The breathing stops. Off-stage an alarm clock rings.
Neighbors' voices. A milkman. Daylight. K wakes, stretches,
rises. First notes of the street-song. The setting flies up and
disappears. Passers-by lift the furniture like sleep-walkers.
The curtain wall is lowered. Downstage of it, children are
playing skittles or marbles. K appears downstage left. He
asks of someone who appears at door A:

K

Carpenter Lanz, please.

MAN

Not here.

K

(Before door B)
Carpenter Lanz?

MAN

(Before door B)
Don't know him.

K

(To the children)
Can you tell me . . . Carpenter Lanz?

CHILDREN

What do you want with him? Go 'way, you're spoiling our game.

(K goes toward door C, which is opening. A woman comes out, her hands covered with soapsuds.)

K

(To the Laundress)
Carpenter Lanz, please?

LAUNDRESS

(Hardly looking at him.)
Ah, the password! You're the one coming for interrogation.
(She goes in again. The whole wall rises slowly and opens on a great vaulted hall. At middle of stage left there is a small platform on which stand a table and two chairs; and on the table there is a pile of books and papers.
The Laundress returns to her washing and pulls her laundry out of a large basket, rinses it and wrings it out.)

LAUNDRESS

(Without looking up at him, going on with her work:)
There's no session today.
(She looks at K, who obviously appeals to her, since she smiles at him; she changes her mind:)
Can I say something to the Examining Magistrate for you?

K

Do you know him?

LAUNDRESS

Oh, yes. My husband is the Court Bailiff. We live here free of charge. It works out very well for us. But we have to clear

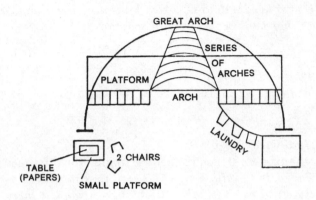

out on the days the court is in session. And afterwards there's a lot to clean.

K

Do they hold sessions often?

LAUNDRESS

Yes, but you never know when. They've arrested you, have they?

K

Yes. But I don't take it very seriously.

LAUNDRESS
You ought to.

K

It's clearly a mistake.

LAUNDRESS

Maybe not. Even if it is a mistake, it's up to you to prove it.

K

Well, of course, I'll have to defend myself.

LAUNDRESS

I might be able to help you. Come sit next to me.

K

With pleasure.

LAUNDRESS

You have lovely dark eyes. Tell me: have you been interrogated already?

K

No, not yet.

LAUNDRESS

Because they often have little preliminary sessions. But they don't let me help in those. Just the same, I learn a lot of things from the Examining Magistrate.

K

You're on friendly terms with him?

LAUNDRESS

He cares a lot for me. I can prove it. Look at those stockings he gave me. He didn't dare bring them himself, so he had the student give them to me.

K

What student?

LAUNDRESS

He works with him and they're close friends. I'm amazed you
don't know him. He comes here all the time.

K

But this is the first time I've been here.

LAUNDRESS
(Surprised)
No! Oh well, you know . . .

K

What?

LAUNDRESS

Nothing.

K

What does he come for?

LAUNDRESS

He says it's to work and to study the records, because afterwards he reports to the Magistrate. That's why he's called the
Student. And also he comes to take me to the Magistrate.

K

And your husband, the Bailiff, what does he say?

LAUNDRESS

Nothing. He's too afraid of losing his job.

44

K

And you?

LAUNDRESS

Well these are very nice stockings, you know. Pure silk.

K

I think they must send you a summons.

LAUNDRESS

No, but that doesn't stop the Magistrate from telling you
first that you're late.

K

But then how do you know when to appear?

LAUNDRESS

You almost never know. That's why there are always so many
waiting. Sometimes for months, sometimes for years.

K

Who waits for what?

LAUNDRESS

For the chance to get in. But I like you very much, and I
might find out from the student . . . Look, here he is. He's
going to pretend he's reading. But he'll watch us. No, go on,
(She means "Go on caressing me.")
as if he weren't there. That beast. Look at those crooked
knees and those twisted legs. There now! He's motioning
for me to come to him.

K

Don't go.

LAUNDRESS

I must. But listen, I'll come back right away, and I'll follow you anywhere you please. You can do whatever you like with me. Oh, all I want is to get out of here for good, never come back.

(She goes on caressing K's hand, or his forehead, and he makes a futile gesture to stop her. She joins the student at the window. K drums on the platform impatiently with his fingers, then with his fist. The student pays no attention and holds the Laundress in his arms. K strides up and down more and more quickly.)

STUDENT

If you're in such a hurry, why don't you leave? Nobody's keeping you. If you had any decency you'd go now—and quick.

K

(Smiling)

Yes, I'm in a hurry. But I'm waiting for you to go. Unless you came to study—then you stay and I'll leave with the lady. My guess is you have a lot of studying to do before you become a judge. I'm not much on legal training, but it must have something to teach you besides insulting people the way you just insulted me.

STUDENT

(To the Laundress)

They shouldn't have let him go about free. It was a mistake. I told the Examining Magistrate so. At least they should have confined him to his room between examinations. There are times when I just don't understand the Magistrate.

46

K

I think we've talked enough.
(He stretches his hand out to the woman.)
Now, you, come with me.

STUDENT

Oh, no! No, you won't get her!
(The Student, showing unsuspected strength, lifts the Laundress to his shoulders like a sack, and leaves. She, over the Student's shoulder, stroking K's face, says:)

LAUNDRESS

You see, I can't do anything. This little beast won't let go of me.

K

(Runs after the two.)
Don't you want to be freed?
(The Student, carrying the woman away, goes up the staircase.)

LAUNDRESS

No, no, of course not. What are you thinking of? It would be the end of me, and of you. Leave him alone. He's only following the Examining Magistrate's orders and taking me to him.

(K climbs several steps painfully in pursuit of them.)

K

Then go ahead! Run, both of you! And I hope I never see you again. Go to the devil!
*(He hits the Student hard.
The Student and the Laundress disappear. K comes down the steps unsteadily, wanders about for a moment in the hall and stops before a sign which catches his eye.)*

K

Hm? "Judicial Archives."
(The Bailiff comes in from below.)

BAILIFF

You haven't seen my wife, have you?

K

You're the Bailiff, of course?

BAILIFF

And you, the defendant, K. How are you?
(He offers his hand and K takes it. The man sits down. He has a pair of slippers in his hand which he laces, after having taken off his shoes.)

K

I know, I spoke to your wife for only a moment. But a student carried her off to the Examining Magistrate.

BAILIFF

Yes. They carry her off all the time. It's Sunday, and I don't have to work today, but they ask me to do all sorts of useless things to get me out of the way. But they're careful not to send me too far, so that I always hope to get back in time. I run like the very devil. I shout my message from the door, so out of breath that people can hardly understand me. I get back as fast as I can, but that student always gets here first. Of course he doesn't have such a long way to go. He just has to come down from the garret. If I weren't such a slave, I would have crushed him against the wall long ago. No! Here, right beside the sign. I dream about it all the time. I see him there, flattened out, nailed up, arms crossed, his fingers straight out, pierced, spurting blood.

K

Can't you think of another way?

BAILIFF

No, none. And it's getting worse. At first, he just took my wife to his own room. Now he takes her to the Examining Magistrate.

K

What about your wife? Doesn't she have anything to say?

BAILIFF

Yes, of course. She's really most to blame. She throws herself at him. The Judge runs after all the women. In this house alone, he's been thrown out of five apartments. Unfortunately he's particularly interested in my wife. She's the best looking one in the house. And I'm the very one who can't defend myself.

K

Why not?

BAILIFF

Because I would have to get rid of the student first. He's a coward. I ought to give him such a walloping when he goes after her that he would lose his taste for her, for even looking at her again. But I haven't the right, and no one else is in a hurry to give me that satisfaction. He's the Judge's pet, and everyone here's afraid of him. Someone like you could do it.

K

Like me? Why?

BAILIFF

Because you're up for trial, that's why.

K

But that's exactly why I would be afraid.

BAILIFF

In the sort of trial they have here, nothing can change the outcome anyhow.

K

Won't you let me believe that . . .

BAILIFF

You can if you want to. I've got to go to the office, now. Would you like to come with me?

K

What would I do there?

BAILIFF ·

You could see the archives and take a look at the people who are waiting. It would teach you something. I think you'd find it interesting.

K

All right, I'll go with you.
(He stops the Bailiff for a moment.)
Listen, what you want to do to that student . . . I'll bet lots of people who work here deserve the same thing.

BAILIFF

Oh, all of them, yes. All.

K

And more than one Judge.

BAILIFF

(Inoffensively)

Oh, a man can't help being rebellious nowadays.

(During these last exchanges, K, following the Bailiff, climbs the steps painfully. They disappear one after the other at the top of the landing. The light changes. A small curtain under the arch of the platform is drawn and reveals the deep perspective of a passageway, actually a stifling tunnel. The corridor is lined with wooden benches on which a great number of people are sitting. The Bailiff and K appear from the rear. K is finishing a sentence.)

K

. . . they really have no consideration for the public.
(K and the Bailiff stop in the midst of the defendants.)

BAILIFF

Consideration! Absolutely none. Just look at this waiting room.
(Everyone gets up as the Bailiff and K walk through.)

K

The humiliations they must have suffered.

BAILIFF

Yes. Everyone you see here, every single one of them is accused.

K

(Ironically)
Yes, my colleagues.

(To the Bailiff)
What are they doing here?

BAILIFF

Waiting.

K

(Politely to one of the defendants)
What are you waiting for, sir?
(The man questioned is upset.)

BAILIFF

This gentleman is only asking you what you're waiting for.
Answer him.

MAN

I am waiting for . . .
(Indistinct, he is interrupted by another Bailiff.)

OTHER BAILIFF

Get out of the way, out of the way! Clear the passage!
(Several of the defendants have gathered around them.)

MAN

I sent a petition to the Court a few months ago, and I'm
waiting for them to act on it.

K

You've gone to a great deal of trouble, haven't you? Is all
that necessary?

MAN

I don't know exactly. I've submitted the documents . . .

K

You don't seem to realize that I'm accused too.

MAN

Oh yes, sir, of course.

K

Don't you believe me?
(He grabs the man's arm; the man lets out a sharp cry.)

MAN

But of course, sir, I do believe you. Just the same that's no
reason to . . .

FIRST BAILIFF

Most of the defendants have become so sensitive . . .

K

I wanted to be sure I wasn't dreaming.
(Laughter and noise, but restrained.)

CHORUS OF THE DEFENDANTS

He's a newcomer . . .
Why doesn't he take his place . . .
He isn't used to it yet . . .
He won't be slow to catch on . . .
Each one waits his turn . . .
He still has to learn . . .
They all have to learn soon enough . . .

K

(Becoming suffocated)
I'd like to go now.

53

BAILIFF

You haven't seen everything yet.

K

I don't want to see everything. I've seen enough.

BAILIFF

Well, you're not lost. Just turn the corner and go along the corridor until you reach the door. You can't miss it.

K

Please come with me and show me the way. There are so many . . . I'm afraid I'll get lost.

BAILIFF

No, there's only one way out. I've wasted too much time with you already. I have a message to deliver.

K

(Desperate)
Don't leave me.

(The Bailiff has gone. Again there is laughter, louder than before.)

CHORUS OF THE DEFENDANTS:

He's come here for the first time . . .
Must just keep quiet . . .
Must wait like us . . .
It's unbelievable that they can't wait quietly any more . . .
When we're thinking of our troubles we don't want to be bothered by . . .
The attendants shouldn't let these things happen . . .
We ought to complain to the authorities about this . . .

Either get out or be quiet, sir . . .
(A young girl comes up, having noticed K's distress.)

YOUNG GIRL

May I help you?
(Understanding K's discomfort, she brings him a chair and forces him to sit down.)
You feel dizzy, don't you? That almost always happens the first time. The sun beats so on this roof. This isn't a very good place for offices, even though it has its good points. There are days here when you can hardly breathe. But after a while you get used to it. When you come back for the third or fourth time . . . Come! You feel better now, don't you? Wait, I'll open the transom.
(A downpour of dust and soot)

ANOTHER BAILIFF

(Turning to K)
You can't stay here. You're holding up traffic. If you're ill, I'll take you to the sickroom.
(He turns to an employee.)
Help me carry this gentleman.

K

(Terrified, stands up suddenly.)
No, no, don't do that . . . I can walk now.
(He takes three steps and falters.)

(Downstage left, an elegant gentleman with a flute-like voice.)

ELEGANT GENTLEMAN

I take it the air here is making this gentleman ill. The best

thing would be not to take him to the sickroom, but to get
him out of these offices.

K

Yes, that's it! That's it! Get out . . . not so weak . . . just a
little help on either arm . . . to the door . . . I'll sit awhile
on the steps . . . and then up again . . . first time ever happened . . . awfully surprised . . . I'm really quite used to office
air . . . but here it's really too much.

ELEGANT GENTLEMAN
(Laughing)
You see.
(To the Young Girl)
I was right. It's this place that makes the gentleman ill. He'll
be all right outside. I'd be delighted to escort the gentleman.

YOUNG GIRL
(Confidentially to K)
Don't let his laughing bother you. He's our Information
Chief, so he has to have an answer for everything. But that's
not his only distinction. He's also a very elegant man. We
thought that the Information Chief had to be dressed smartly
to impress the public. He's the one people see first. The rest
of us are all much more sloppily dressed. Why spend any
money on clothes when we never leave these offices? We even
sleep here. But we thought the Information Chief should
have a handsome suit of clothes. The Administration didn't
agree with us, so we made a collection ourselves to buy him
the outfit he's wearing.

ELEGANT GENTLEMAN
Why, my dear girl, do we have to tell this gentleman all our
secrets? They can hardly interest him.

YOUNG GIRL

I had to explain to him why you laughed. It might have offended him.

ELEGANT GENTLEMAN

I think this gentleman will forgive us everything if we only get him out. Come! Get up, you poor, delicate man! This way. Now: here's your fresh air!

K

Ah! Thank you. Many thanks.

A sudden infiltration of crude light. The group with K goes out as the curtain falls.

END OF FIRST PART

SECOND PART

SCENE ONE

Scene: Bank Office. K is finishing dictating a letter.

K

. . . centralizes the authority here, and takes the matter out
of my hands. That's all.

FEMALE EMPLOYEE

Signature, sir?
(K signs some papers. A hnock at the door.)

K

Come in!
*(Two employees enter. K's uncle edges his way in behind
them. K doesn't see him at once. He is busy signing papers.
A moment passes. K makes a gesture to let him finish.
Finally, looking up, he sees his uncle.)*
Ah, uncle!
(He gets up. His uncle embraces him.)

UNCLE

Well, you're certainly protected. I had a hard time getting
in to see you. I know you're busy, but I've got to talk to you.
I came in from the country just for that.

(K gestures for him to be seated. The Uncle pulls his chair close to K. The employees take two steps forward.)

UNCLE

I'd like to speak to you alone.

K

(To employees)
Come back later when this gentleman is gone. I'll call you.
I don't want to be disturbed.

UNCLE

I'll take as little of your time as possible.

K

(Wearily, making an effort to smile)
Well, what good angel brings you here?

UNCLE

(Shaking his head)
Good angel? My boy, tell me at once, is there any truth in
this story?

K

What story? Really, uncle, I don't know what you're talking
about.

UNCLE

Joseph, Joseph, you always told me the truth till now. Have
you changed? Why didn't you tell me about your trial. It
isn't a criminal trial, is it?

K

(Shrugging his shoulders)

Yes, it is.
(He rises very calmly and raises the shade to look out of the window.)

UNCLE

And you sit here calmly with a criminal trial on your hands? This isn't exactly the time to stand looking out the window!

K

The calmer I am, the better it is for me. Don't worry about me.

UNCLE

But, my boy, it's not you alone. Think of your relatives and your family's good name. We've always been proud of you; don't disgrace us now. Hurry up and tell me what happened. It's something at the bank, of course.

K

No. But you're talking much too loudly. There's always someone listening behind doors.
(He walks up to his uncle, and before sitting down again:)
I know very well I owe the family an explanation.
(He sits down and in a confidential tone:)
First of all, Uncle, you must understand that this isn't a trial before an ordinary court.

UNCLE

That's bad.

K

Why?

UNCLE

I just say it's bad. Listen, my boy, you look tired. You've

63

gotten thin. What you need is a vacation. Come and stay with
us in the country for a few days.

K

They wouldn't let me go.

UNCLE

Who are they?

K

I wish I knew!

UNCLE

Joseph, you've changed. You've always been clear about
things, and now you're confused. Do you want to lose your
case? Do you realize what it would mean? You'd be an out-
cast, and the whole family along with you. In any case, it
would be the worst kind of humiliation. Joseph I beg of
you, snap out of it. It's maddening to see you so indifferent!

K

Being excited doesn't do any good. It's no way to win a trial.
I was hoping you'd think the whole thing even less important than I do. Apparently it upsets you more. I've always
listened to you; but going to the country doesn't seem very
sensible. It would look as if I were running away, and they
would take it as a confession. To run away would be to
admit my guilt.

UNCLE

Are you guilty?

K

(After a moment)
I don't think so.

UNCLE

But you must know.

K

I don't know. I don't know any more.

UNCLE

How can that be?

K

I won't get much of a rest from them staying here, I can tell you, but I'll be in a better position to prepare my case.

UNCLE

Very well, I only suggested it because I saw you throwing away your case by your indifference, and if you did, it would be better to take over for you. But if you're ready to put yourself into it with all your heart . . .

K

What do you think I should do first?

UNCLE

First off—right away—we'll look up Mr. Huld, the Advocate. He's an old classmate of mine. You've probably heard of him . . . No? That's odd. Anyhow he's a famous defense lawyer and advocate for the poor. But most of all it's the man in him that inspires my confidence.

K

I didn't think I'd have to take an Advocate for a matter of this kind.

66

UNCLE

Of course you must! Why shouldn't you take one. Let's go there this evening. We'll be sure to find him in.

(They go.)

Meanwhile, you can tell me everything that's happened up to now.

(They have gone, but they are still audible.)

I'll have to be briefed completely on the whole affair.

END OF SCENE ONE

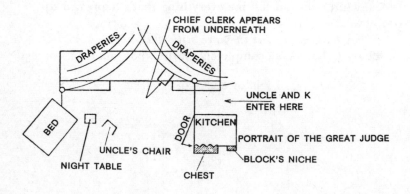

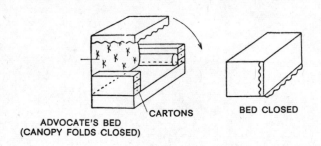

ADVOCATE'S BED
(CANOPY FOLDS CLOSED)

SCENE TWO

At the Advocate's. A knocking at the Advocate's door is heard in the wings.

LENI (THE MAID)

The Advocate is ill. He's in bed and can't see anyone.
(She returns to the bedside, holding a wax candle in one hand, and a cup of tea in the other.)

UNCLE

(Off stage)
That's the new maid, she's afraid of strangers.
(Another knock)

ADVOCATE

(To the maid)
Find out who it is, anyhow.

UNCLE

Open up, open up. We're friends of the Advocate.
(Leni opens the door, holding the candle in her hand.)

UNCLE

Come on, Joseph.

LENI

The Advocate is ill.

UNCLE

It's his heart, isn't it?

LENI

I think so.

ADVOCATE

I would like to know, though . . .

UNCLE

(From off stage)
It's Albert. Your old friend. Come on, Joseph.

ADVOCATE

Albert. Ah, my friend. I'm in a bad way.

*(The Uncle, who has taken the candle from Leni's hand,
brings it close to the Advocate.)*

UNCLE

It's your heart trouble again, I suppose. You've had this
before; you'll get over it; you always have.

ADVOCATE

It's worse than the other times. I can't sleep, I can hardly
breathe. I'm losing more strength every day.

UNCLE

Are they taking good care of you? It's so dismal in here,
so dark! I seem to remember that the house used to be more
gay. Your little miss has a dismal way about her too, or
maybe it only seems so.

70

ADVOCATE

When you're as ill as I am, you don't want any gaiety. And
Leni takes very good care of me. She is sweet.
  (Leni adjusts his pillows.)

UNCLE

Would you leave us for a moment, please, Miss? I must discuss a personal matter with my friend.

LENI

You can see that the Advocate is in no condition now to
bother about your personal affairs.

UNCLE

I haven't lost my reason, Miss. If what I ask weren't possible, I wouldn't ask it. Now leave us, please.

ADVOCATE

You can say anything you want in front of Leni.

UNCLE

I'm not here about my own affairs, but my nephew's. May
I introduce you: Mr. Joseph K, Assistant Bank Manager . . .

ADVOCATE

Please forgive me, sir, I hadn't noticed you.
  (To Leni)
Go, my child. Leave us.
  *(He presses her hand as though he were saying good-bye for
  a long time.)*
You haven't come then to visit a sick friend, but on this
business of your nephew's.

71

UNCLE

You seem much better already now that that little witch
has gone. I'll bet she listens at the door.

ADVOCATE

Oh, you're wrong about her. She's better than you think . . .
As far as your nephew's business is concerned, I'm very much
interested in it, but I don't know whether I'll have the
strength for such a difficult job. I feel I'm just not up to it
. . . After all, if I can't do it alone, there will always be time
to call in a colleague. To be perfectly frank, this case interests me too much to refuse to take it on personally.

K

I don't understand how you . . .

ADVOCATE

Am I mistaken? My eagerness may have put me on the
wrong track . . .
(To K)
I thought this was about your trial . . .

UNCLE

Of course.
(To K)
What's the matter with you?

K

How do you know anything about me or about my trial?

ADVOCATE

Ah, that's what's bothering you. But you know that I'm an
Advocate. Your uncle must have told you. In that capacity,
I'm in contact with the people of the Law Courts. We al-

ways talk about the trials, and we always remember the most striking ones; especially, if one happens to involve the nephew of a friend. There's nothing very surprising in that, it seems to me.

UNCLE

(To K)
What else do you expect? You look puzzled.

K

You move in the circles of the Law Courts?

ADVOCATE

Certainly!

K

Mr. Advocate, Carpenter Lanz, could you tell me who he is?

ADVOCATE

(Closing up)
I don't have to know him, and it's of no importance.

UNCLE

You ask questions like a child.

ADVOCATE

Of course, my illness is a great obstacle to me at the moment; but there are always friends who come to see me. They're connected with the Court, and from them I learn many things. In fact, there's someone very close to me from the Court who's here right now.

K

Where?

*(The Uncle has risen, holding the candle. From behind
the curtain at the rear the Chief Clerk of the Court comes
out, embarrassed at attracting so much attention. He approaches, bowing repeatedly.)*

ADVOCATE

Ah, you've come in just as we were . . . But first I must
introduce you: Albert K, my old friend, and his nephew,
Bank Manager Joseph K . . . And this is the Chief Clerk
of the Court.

(Salutations and handshakes.)

The Chief Clerk was kind enough to come tonight to bring
me up to date on news at the Court. A layman can't really
appreciate the significance of his visits. You would have to
be one of us. You must be aware, certainly, of the immense
amount of work that accumulates for so distinguished a man.
And in spite of his work, he comes to see me. We were in
the midst of going over a very interesting case, and as I
didn't expect anyone, Leni hadn't been given instructions . . .
When we heard you knock, the Chief Clerk retired. But
you'll profit from his information if he's kind enough . . .
For the case we were studying, I confess, is yours.

CHIEF CLERK

Unfortunately, I have just a few minutes, and then I must
go. But I shouldn't want to miss the chance to meet a friend
of a friend of mine. Then, too, the matter that brings you
here seems to me to be particularly worthy of our attention.

(Speaks more and more quickly.)

Now your case has the special virtue of being of particular
interest, and at the same time, it has, so to speak—more general interest. If I may say so, it touches at the same time on
public morality and on private conduct. On this question
I permitted myself to point out to our friend the singular

delaying factors and detours, and I should say the "undulating" features, to which the ordinary processes of law force us to have recourse. Now let us take an instance in which . . .

(Noise of breaking crockery comes from the kitchen. The conversation stops abruptly. K, who had stopped listening, rises at once: a good chance to get away.)

K

I'll see what's happened.
(He hurries to join Leni in the kitchen. The three gentlemen continue the conversation, but one hardly hears them. The light dims at left, and goes up at right.)

LENI

I threw a plate against the wall hoping that it would make you come out. I wanted to speak to you.

K

I wanted to talk to you too. But I'm a little shy . . . and you seemed to be so reserved . . .

LENI

Let's sit down here, all right? I was afraid you wouldn't like me.

K

Oh, "like" is too mild a word.

LENI

Really? Then call me Leni from now on. Would you like to?

K

I'd love to, Leni.

(Furtive caresses.
K points to an enormous portrait which covers the panel
above the kitchen.)
Whose portrait is that?

LENI

It's one of the Judges.

K

One of the great Magistrates?

LENI

(Laughing)
Certainly not! He's a little nobody of an Examining Magistrate. I know him very well. He comes here often. He likes
to look big in the picture because he's so vain. They're all
like that. I'm vain too, and I'm annoyed that you don't
like me more.

K

It isn't true, Leni! Don't think that! . . .
(Caresses redouble, but his mind is elsewhere.)
What rank does he have?

LENI

I just told you. He's only an Examining Magistrate. The
really great Judges, no one ever sees them.

K

But he's sitting in such a big armchair.

LENI

(Laughing)

In the picture, yes. Actually, it's a kitchen chair, with a horse-blanket folded in four.
(Strange noises are heard from extreme right.)

K

Who's making that noise?

LENI

That? That's Block; the merchant Block.
(A little old man appears, with a scraggly beard. He is squatting and half crawls to them, holding a candle and an old dirty briefcase.)

K

What is he doing herc?

LENI

Oh, don't get excited. He's waiting.

K

Is he your lover?
(Leni laughs.)

LENI

You're not going to be jealous of Block! . . . All right, Rudi, leave your candle here.
(She takes the candlestick from him.)

K

And . . . he sleeps here?

BLOCK

I don't see why you should be jealous.

LENI

(To K)

I'll explain it to you. Block is a big client of the Advocate's. But since the Advocate usually calls him in the middle of the night, he sleeps here.

K

In this hole!

LENI

And I take care of him a little when the Advocate can't see him.

BLOCK

And that's a big help.

VOICE OF THE ADVOCATE

Leni!

LENI

Oh! I forgot about his eggnog! Don't go, I'll be back.

(While Leni goes to the Advocate's bed, the two men study one another. K, with a glance toward the room at the side, draws Block close to the chest on which K is seated. Block squats at his feet.)

K

So, Mr. Block, you're a faithful old client of the Advocate's, are you?

BLOCK

A very old client, perfectly true. As for the faithfulness . . .

K

What do you mean?

BLOCK

Nothing.
(Correcting himself)
Promise first not to betray me.

K

How can you know I won't?

BLOCK

No, I think you won't. You don't look like a betrayer. And it
does me so much good to be able to talk to someone. Well,
listen: besides Mr. Huld, I have five other Advocates.

K

Five?

BLOCK

Sh . . . And I'm negotiating now for a sixth.

K

That doesn't seem so terrible to me.

BLOCK

Terrible? Maybe not. But it's forbidden; especially if they're
low back-alley lawyers. Now, please don't tell anyone.

K

But why so many Advocates?

BLOCK

I need all of them, all of them. Since they don't all have the
same point of view, they don't all give me the same advice.
(Pathetically)
I don't want to lose my case. I've spent everything I have,

79

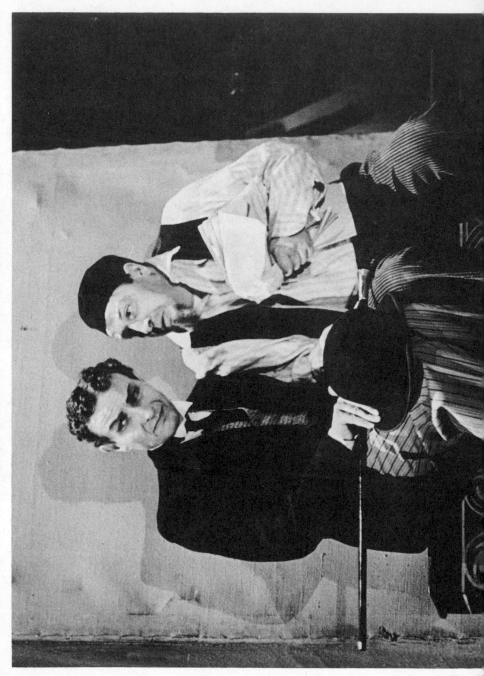

all my strength, all my time on my case. Every day as soon as
they let me leave here, I run to the offices of the Court.

K

But what do you do there?

BLOCK

Oh! Nothing. I'm simply there. I wait. Just the fact of sitting
there and waiting my turn, that in itself requires a great
effort.

K

And there's nothing better to do?

BLOCK

No, unless you try to hurry things.

K

What do you mean, to hurry things?

BLOCK

I don't know exactly. And by now it's too late for me to ask
that question. As for hurrying, I think you must decide for
it right away.

K

You do?

BLOCK

Yes; before you've gotten into the habit.

K

What habit?

BLOCK

Of waiting. Even so, it was out of a desire to hurry things
that I took on the others, the alley-lawyers . . . because it was
impossible to talk to the great ones.

K

(Coming closer to him)
What do you mean? Tell me. All this interests me tre-
mendously.

BLOCK

Mr. Huld, when he talks of himself or his colleagues, says:
we great Advocates. Well that isn't true. They are only little,
very little Advocates. The great ones, the really great ones,
you can never see.

(Leni comes back to the kitchen with the empty cup.)

K

But are you absolutely sure that . . .

BLOCK

. . . that they are as far above them as those here are above
the back-alley lawyers, whom they talk about with such
contempt.

K

Even without seeing them, haven't you tried to get hold of
them?

BLOCK

Of course I have, but not for very long! And since then
I can't stop thinking about them. It's a thought that plagues
me, especially at night, or in the waiting rooms, in the
corridors.

*(Close to the bed of the Advocate, the Chief Clerk is seen
rising and taking his leave. The Uncle is visibly embarrassed, and looks to the right and left to see whether
K is returning. Leni leaves the kitchen again.)*

LENI

You two have certainly gotten into a huddle.

BLOCK

He asked me to tell him about my trial.

LENI

(To K)
All you can think about is your trial.

K

Not at all. I probably don't think about it enough.

LENI

(On her knees)
I've heard that you're too stubborn.

K

Who told you that?

LENI

Don't ask me his name; but try to get over it. It doesn't do
you any good. You have no weapons against the Law. It's better to confess right away, believe me.

K

But confess what?

LENI

Well, that's your affair. It's only after confession that you can

try to escape. Only after; and you succeed only if someone
helps you.
(To Block, who, squatting, pulls hairs out of the carpet.)
Rudi, leave that skin alone . . . I'll be glad to try to help you.
(They fall down on the carpet.)
Oh, you've kissed me.

*(Block goes back to his corner. Meanwhile, the Uncle is
seen. He is utterly distressed at not seeing his nephew
return; he takes leave of the Advocate, apologizing to him.
He goes out downstage left.)*

LENI

(To K)
And now you must hurry back to the old man. Here, take
the house-key. Come whenever you want to.
*(She goes back into the kitchen.
K straightens his clothes and rejoins his uncle as he is
leaving.)*

UNCLE

There you are, you! That was a fine thing to do to us in
there! We bother to take so much interest in your case, and
you carry on as though it doesn't matter to you at all.

K

But my dear Uncle . . .

UNCLE

Don't "dear Uncle" me. You've acted like an absolute boor,
and if the family weren't so much implicated, and . . .
(The rest is lost.)

(They reappear.)
. . . and without even looking for an excuse, to go off and

hide with a little trollop, who, to make it worse, is obviously
the Advocate's mistress. And you leave us sitting there, all
three of us, your uncle wearing himself out for you, an
Advocate, who is only trying to help you, and the Chief Clerk
of the Court, a powerful man, who can do so much for your
trial in its present stage. We try to find some way to help
you. I have to handle the Advocate with silk gloves, and the
Advocate has to kowtow to the Chief Clerk, and then the
Chief Clerk himself . . .

(They leave.)

(They reappear under the same umbrella.)

*During the coming and going of K and the Uncle down-
stage—they are in the street—the setting is partially trans-
formed under a light change. To the left of the Advocate's
room, only the monumental bed remains. On the right,
nothing of the kitchen area remains except for the chest on
which K and Leni were sitting, Block's niche and the large
portrait of the Great Judge, which dominates the scene.
In the frame, during a quick dimming of the lights, a real
Judge has replaced the painted figure. In the center, on the
platform which is seen again, we see the props of K's office
—the desk and chair.*

*This scene, then, is composed of four units which appear
simultaneously, separately at first; and finally merging.*

A—The Advocate's bed

B—Block's niche

C—The Judge in the frame

D—K's office at the bank

85

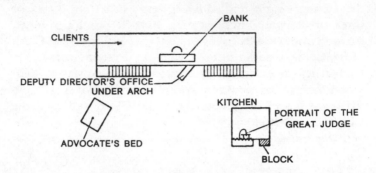

(Interrupting the Uncle's first speech to K, and during their momentary exit, while they are walking along the proscenium street, the Advocate says to Leni, who is fixing his bed, at A:)

ADVOCATE

No, don't try to make excuses for him. When he's in such trouble, the least he could do is listen to us. The Chief Clerk of the Court himself! An incredible kindness . . .
(The rest is lost. The Uncle and K reappear.)

UNCLE

You can imagine how relieved I was when he went. I could hardly breathe. The Advocate, who was ill to begin with, took it even harder. He was hardly able to say good-bye to me when I left. Such a fine man! You've probably pushed him into his decline. You've brought the one man who was your greatest hope to his grave. What more can I say?

ADVOCATE

(To Leni, A:)
What more can I say?

UNCLE

(At proscenium)

Nothing. I think it's useless, and you're in enough trouble anyway . . . Let's go. I'll leave you here . . . You have enough to do, and you mustn't neglect your job at the bank.

(The Uncle says good-bye to K and leaves. K sits down in his office. An employee comes in, at D.)

EMPLOYEE

The Deputy Director would like to know . . .

K

He will have to wait. See to it that I am not disturbed this morning.

ADVOCATE

(At A, shouts:)

Leni, come back to me. Don't leave me alone, child! I don't feel well. This business has upset me. I spent most of the night drawing up the petition. How do you like this boy?

LENI

I don't know. I didn't even look at him.

ADVOCATE

Leni, Leni! Don't try to make me out a bigger fool than I am. Don't you think I noticed his absence when he went to look for you in the kitchen? I'm worn out by all this. Bring me a cup of tea, child.

(Leni leaves the Advocate's bed and goes to the kitchen.)

BLOCK

(From his corner, B)

His trial is only in its first stages. It's natural that the Advo-

cate would take pleasure in working on it. But that'll change
soon enough.

ADVOCATE

(From A)
I wouldn't think of giving it up!
(He arranges some papers scattered on his bed.)

K

(From D)
Well, Mr. Advocate, when you send me your bill, you won't
get a penny from me, not a penny.

ADVOCATE

*(Laughs very loudly, as though addressing the Judge's
portrait.)*
That young man seems to think that a trial of this sort can
be handled without an Advocate. What an innocent idea of
the Law people have. Leni, bring the tea.

K

(From D)
An Advocate . . . I'd probably do better hiring another one.
This one my uncle chose is no good.

THE GREAT JUDGE

*(From C
Sententiously, and very loudly:)*
Once the accused chooses an Advocate, he must remain with
him, whatever happens.

K

(From D)
Anyhow, I've nothing to worry about. What charge could
they bring against me?

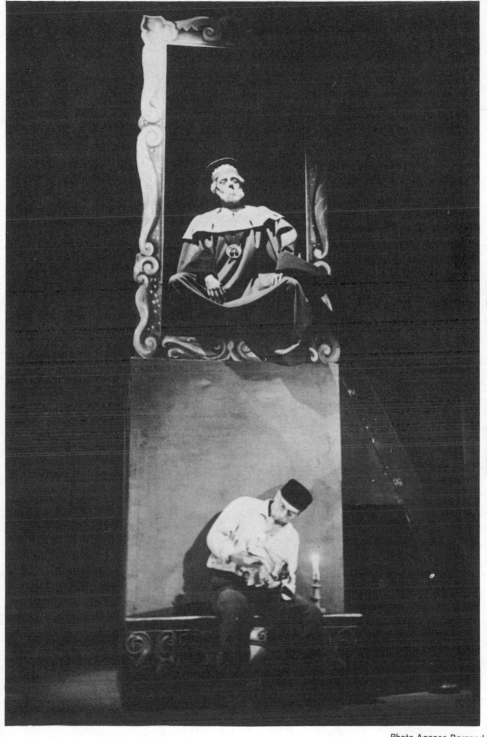

Photo Agence Bernand

ADVOCATE

(Addressing the Great Judge, from A)

You try to make him understand. I give up. He doesn't seem to realize that a defendant is guilty until he proves himself innocent. Leni, find Block.

K

(From D)

How can I prove my innocence if I don't know what I'm accused of?

LENI

(From kitchen, B)

Block! Block! The Advocate wants to see you.

THE GREAT JUDGE

(From C)

The defendant is not to know what he's accused of, at least not before his condemnation.

K

(From D)

Then there's no way out . . . except perhaps through pull, through the right contacts . . .

ADVOCATE

(From A)

What a pity, Joseph, what a pity, that you turned your back on the Chief Clerk, such an important man. You behaved like an oaf.

(A messenger from the bank comes in, addressing K, at D)

MESSENGER

If the Manager will forgive me for disturbing him, there are some people who've been waiting for a long time and are getting impatient.

(He leans toward K, and we hear only the end of the sentence.)

. . . one of the bank's most important clients.

K

(Resigned)
Have him come in.

CLIENT

Excuse me, Mr. K, for interrupting your work. It must be very absorbing.

K

I should apologize to you, Sir, for making you wait.

CLIENT

I can explain my business in a few words.

(He takes out a batch of papers from his briefcase, and spreads them on the desk before K, who is distracted.)
It isn't very complicated. You remember that you helped me work out a contract last year with my partner. Everything would have been fine if I hadn't found out—a little too late, I'm afraid—that my partner, who I thought was an honest man . . .

(While the client continues to talk, K remains lost in thought and continues to watch what is happening at the Advocate's bed.)

ADVOCATE

(To Leni, at A.)
How has Block been behaving today?

LENI

He's been quiet, and he's worked. I shut him up in his little room so he wouldn't bother me.

K

(At D)
In his hole, like a dog.

LENI

I could see him through the transom. He crouched on his bed and he never stopped reading the documents you gave him. He put them on the sill of the transom so he could see better. That made a good impression on me.

ADVOCATE

Was he studying his case?

LENI

Only once he called to me that he was thirsty. I gave him a glass of water. At eight o'clock I fed him.

CLIENT

(At D)
You see what I mean, don't you?

K

(Distracted)
I can't believe it!

CLIENT

What can't you believe? I haven't told you anything yet.

92

K

No, but I can guess.

(Block stays at the foot of the Advocate's bed in his begging posture.)

LENI

He would like to know what the third Judge told you.

ADVOCATE

He did not pronounce favorably either on Block himself or his trial.

LENI

Not favorably! Is that possible?

ADVOCATE

He looked displeased the moment I began to talk about Block. "Don't talk to me about Block," he said. "He's my client," I said. "You're letting him take advantage of you," he answered. "I don't believe it," I said, "Block is spending a lot of effort on his trial. He practically lives in my house, ready for me to call him at any time. Of course, he's quite disagreeable. He has revolting manners, he's dirty, unusually so; but I can't complain about his attitude toward his trial." I put it as strongly as I could, but he answered, "Block is sly. He has learned a lot of tricks, and he knows how to drag out his case. But when you get right down to it, he doesn't know anything. What would he say if he knew that his trial hasn't even begun yet, and that the bell hasn't rung yet for the opening session?"

(During all this, K pretends to be absorbed in reading his client's papers, but he looks toward the Advocate from time to time.)

93

K

(At D)

If he thinks he can get at me with these antics he's mistaken.

CLIENT

Mr. Manager, you're apparently not yourself just now. This
has been a stormy day. You seem to be preoccupied.

K

Yes, I have a headache . . . family troubles.

CLIENT

Yes. Each of us has his cross to bear. To get back to this
matter . . .

K

Would you excuse me just a moment?
*(He gets up and goes to the Advocate's bed. The Deputy
Director, having waited for just this moment, rushes over
to the client, and he tries to whisper to him.)*

K

(At A)

Considering the state of your health, I came to tell you that
I'm relieving you of the burden of my case.

ADVOCATE

Do I understand what you're saying?

K

I think you do.

ADVOCATE

This is very interesting. It's a proposal we'll have to consider.

K

It's not a proposal any more.

ADVOCATE

I understand, but it's most important not to rush things.

K

I'm not rushing things. I've considered the whole matter, and my decision is final.

ADVOCATE

In that case, let me make one or two suggestions.

K

Just a moment, Mr. Advocate.
(He hurries back to his office where the Deputy Director is conversing with the Client with excessive amiability.)

DEPUTY DIRECTOR

(At D)
. . . very important. I understand perfectly.
(And while the Client gathers his papers, and gives them to him)
The Manager will be delighted, I'm sure, that we relieved him of this matter. He's flooded with work and he's been looking very tired the last few days. Would you step into my office?
(They go out.)

CLIENT

(To K, as he passes him.)
I'll be back, Mr. Manager. I have something I must tell you before I leave.
(K nods dully.)

ADVOCATE

(At A)

Come now, young man. You can see for yourself you're no
longer able to carry on your daily work. This trial is important enough for you to give it your full energy and attention.

THE GREAT JUDGE

(At C)

Only a detailed defense would do any good. And that requires
sacrificing all other work.

BLOCK

(From his corner)

Once my business offices took up the whole ground floor of
a large building. Now I'm satisfied in a small room at the
end of the corridor.

THE GREAT JUDGE

(At C)

A provisional arrest, it's true, but nobody can foresee how
long it will last.

BLOCK

(At B)

It's not the loss of money that's brought me to this, but really
the weakening of my faculties, of my power to work.

K

(At D. Goes to wash his hands in the sink.)

I must keep my mind clear. Maybe I didn't take it all seriously enough at first.

*(He goes over to the window to open it. The Client re-
turns.)*

CLIENT

A bad autumn.

*(He follows K's glance which rests on the Client's briefcase
stuffed with papers.)*

The matter is all settled. A charming man, your Deputy
Director. And such competence!

(K starts to sit down, exhausted.)

CLIENT

Mr. Manager, there's something I must tell you. I'm grateful
for what you've done for me in the past, and I thought I
ought to tell you this. You can make whatever use of it you
please, but I think it will be valuable for you to know.

(He sits down next to K, and says confidentially:)

It's about your trial.

K

The Deputy Director told you.

CLIENT

He could hardly know.

K

But how do you know?

CLIENT

Sometimes I get a little information from the courts. Those
judges are terribly vain. They have their portraits painted
and almost always by the same painter . . . a certain Titorelli.
I'm sure that's not his real name. But while they're sitting
for him, the judges let little secrets fall. Now this painter . . .
I know him very well: I buy some of his pictures occasionally.
A word from me will get him to see you. He's very talkative,
and he'll be able to give you some first-rate advice, and

maybe even intervene with the judges. Certainly on my recommendation, he'll do everything he can for you. You ought to see him.

K

You really think . . .

CLIENT

No obligation, of course. It's just advice I'm giving you. Here, I'll write a note for you. Use it if you want to. May I?
(He walks over to K's desk.)

K

Yes, I think you're right. I'll go to see him right away.
(A messenger comes in while the Client is writing.)

MESSENGER

Excuse me, but there are three clients in the other room who've been waiting some time. They'd like to know if . . .
(From below, the three wearied clients come up—from the left—to the platform. From the passage-way, the Deputy Director watches, and gets ready to join the group.)

THE THREE CLIENTS
(At D)
Mr. Manager . . . No, allow me . . . I was here before you . . . But Sir, I protest, that simply isn't so . . .
(Mild jostling.)

K

Forgive me, gentlemen, I'm very sorry. A thousand pardons. Must leave. Extremely urgent matter. Would you be good enough to come back tomorrow or another day.

ONE OF THE CLIENTS

My business is urgent . . .

ANOTHER

Mine can't be delayed.

(The Deputy Director has come in, and he takes in the situation.)

DEPUTY DIRECTOR

(Very calmly)

Gentlemen, you can all be taken care of very easily. Since our Manager is forced to be away, and we have all the papers here anyway, you will permit me, I think . . .

(He is talking to K.)

to sit at your desk? Of course, only during your absence.

K

(Furious)

Go ahead! Don't bother about me at all! I can't think clearly today, but when I'm myself again, I'll teach you to step on my toes!

END OF SCENE TWO

SCENE THREE

Titorelli's studio. Stairs or corridor. K meets a group of little girls. The first is hunchbacked.

K

Does the painter Titorelli live here?

THE LITTLE GIRLS

What do you want him for?

K

I want him to paint my portrait.

THE LITTLE GIRLS
(Laughing)
Oh! He's a judge!

K

No, I'm not.

THE FIRST GIRL

Then why do you want your picture painted?

K

Mind your own business.

THE FIRST GIRL

Mind yours! Why don't you take a good look at yourself?
You're not very handsome, you know.

K

You're hardly the one to say that.
*(He looks at her with pity. The hunchbacked girl laughs
slyly and meanly.)*

THE FIRST GIRL

Come! Everybody's going to see Tito. This way. Follow me.
*(From door A of the wall emerges suddenly, drawn by the
noise, a man in a nightshirt who disappears at once, saying:*
Oh, excuse me!
*when the hunchbacked girl and the others appear. Panel A
then rises and reveals a little anteroom with another door,
gaily colored, and on which is written TITORELLI.
Titorelli appears, like Daumier's Don Quixote. He has
slipped a pair of long drawers over his nightshirt. His feet
are bare.)*

K

Mr. Titorelli? . . .

TITORELLI

At your service.

*Panels B and C rise and show Titorelli's studio. The walls
are of bare wood. To the right is a canvas, its back three-
quarters to the audience, over which a cloth has been
thrown. A painter's stool. In the back, a folding bedstead
on which are spread brightly colored cushions and quilts.
To the left, a chair, sketches and the door.*

(Pantomime with the little girls whom Titorelli has not succeeded in keeping from coming in with K.)

TITORELLI

Oh! The little pests! . . . Ever since I painted one of them I have them on my neck all the time . . .

(He grabs one whom he throws out; he motions to K to sit down.)

While I'm here I can keep them under control; but they've made a duplicate key for this door and as soon as they know I'm out . . .

(He pursues another of the girls.)

The other day, I come back with a lady whose portrait I'm doing.

(He catches her.)

And what do I find? The little hunchbacked one is standing in front of the paintbox, painting her lips with a brush—

(He throws her out.)

while her brothers and sisters are making a mess in every corner of the room . . . And even last night . . . Excuse the condition of the place.

(Attempt at pursuit, but he gives it up.)

I come back very tired from a day's work outside, and all I want is to go to sleep. The minute I get under the covers, I feel a pinch on the leg. One of those little imps hid under the bed for hours waiting for me to get in.

(He catches the third one by surprise and throws her out; closes the door; the three squeal.)

All they think about is playing tricks on me and every day one or the other thinks up something new. If the Court didn't let me have this studio free, I would have moved out long ago.

ONE OF THE LITTLE GIRLS

Tito, may we come in?

TITORELLI

(In the voice of a bogeyman)
No!

THE FIRST GIRL

Just me, Tito? Can't I come in alone?

TITORELLI

No!
(He turns the key in the door. To K:)
And now, Sir, what can I do for you?

K

(Who has witnessed the whole turmoil with bewilderment, gets hold of himself; he rises.)
I was given your address by this gentleman.
(He hands him the letter of his client.)
And it's on his advice that I came to see you.
(Titorelli runs through the letter unconcernedly and throws it on the bed.)

TITORELLI

Do you want to buy pictures or have your portrait done?

K

Were you just working on a picture?

TITORELLI

Yes.
(He bares the easel, on which a large allegorical painting is resting.)
This is a good painting, you know. Not quite finished yet.

103

K

(Pretending great interest)
Another portrait of a judge?

TITORELLI

Why do you say another?

K

Because I think I've seen others done by you. That large
figure behind the judge, who's that?

TITORELLI

That's Justice.

K

Ah! Yes, yes, yes! I begin to see. Yes, the band over the eyes.
Of course, and there are the scales. But it looks as though
she has wings on her heels . . . as though she wants to take
flight.

TITORELLI

(Turning up his cuffs to work)
I had orders to treat her like that. She's supposed to represent
both Justice and Fortune. You see, I didn't work from any
model; it's simply what I was told to do. He, for instance:
he's only a very little judge, but he insists I show him on a
throne, a great big throne.

K

He certainly looks like an all-powerful judge. And Justice
. . . you would almost take her for the Goddess of the Hunt.

TITORELLI

(Painting all the while)
Wouldn't you?

K

What's his name?

TITORELLI

They don't let me tell you that.

K

I must say, you're a man who really has the Court's confidence.

TITORELLI

Do you think I don't know why you came? You came to talk to me about your trial. The note told me. But to get on the right side of me, you start by talking about my pictures. Well, you're right. I do have their confidence.

K

I hardly know how to ask you, but . . . does it carry any official recognition?

TITORELLI

No.

K

But these semi-official positions sometimes carry more influence than the official ones, . . . don't they?

TITORELLI

In my case, that's true. When I was talking about your trial yesterday to the manufacturer who wrote the note, he asked me if I could help you. I told him all you have to do is come to see me. But frankly I didn't expect you so soon. You take it to heart, this trouble you're in, eh? . . . Don't you want to take off your coat?

THE LITTLE GIRLS

*(Outside; watching through the keyhole and the cracks in
the wall, very excitedly:)*
Oh! He's taking off his overcoat!

TITORELLI

I need lots of warmth for my work. That's one good thing
about this place . . . Sit down on the bed. Oh, don't be embarrassed. Jump in . . . Now tell me first, are you innocent?

K

(Immensely relieved by this question)
Yes.

TITORELLI

Honestly, just between ourselves?

K

I'm completely innocent.

TITORELLI

(Very slowly)
Ah! . . . Ah! . . . Ah! . . .
(He lifts his head abruptly.)
Well, if you're innocent, the case is simple.

K

I certainly thought so at first; but I found out soon enough
that my innocence didn't make it simpler at all.
(Titorelli cannot refrain from smiling. He shakes his head.)
There are so many little by-ways the Law gets lost in! It ends
up by discovering a sin where there's never been one.

TITORELLI

(Meditating)
Surely! Surely! But you're innocent just the same.

K

Yes . . . am I not?

TITORELLI

Well, that's the main thing.

K

Listen, Mr. Titorelli, you surely know the Law better than
I do; I only know it from hearsay. But I've learned that
everyone agrees that an accusation is never lightly initiated,
and that once begun, the Court holds and continues to hold
the accused guilty. I've been told that it's only with the
greatest difficulty you can get them to change their minds.

TITORELLI

Difficulty? My friend, it would be more accurate to say you
never get them to change their minds. If I were to take this
canvas and paint all the judges in the Court on it in a row,
and you were to stand in front of it telling them how innocent you are till the end of your days, you would without the
slightest doubt have more success than pleading your case
before the actual Court.

THE LITTLE GIRLS

Tito, won't he go away soon?

TITORELLI

Be quiet! Can't you see we're in the middle of a conversation?

THE LITTLE GIRLS

Are you going to paint his portrait? . . . Don't. He's too ugly.

TITORELLI

(He goes to the door and half-opens it.)
If you don't shut up and stay shut up, I'll throw every one
of you down that whole flight of stairs! Now sit down on the
steps and don't move.
(He comes back to K.)
I'm sorry. Those dear little things also belong to the Law.

K

How could they?

TITORELLI

There's nothing that doesn't belong to the Law. You don't
seem to understand that yet. Actually though, you don't need
to since you're innocent. You'll get out of it all by yourself.

K

But how would you advise me to go about it? What steps
should I take? From what you told me just now it looks as
though the Court doesn't listen to any kind of proof.

TITORELLI

(Raising his forefinger)
The Court doesn't, that's true. But it's different when you do
it unofficially, through certain intermediaries. . . . Don't be
surprised to hear me talking like a lawyer. It comes from
living close to the Court for so long. Since before I was their
age. *(Indicating the Little Girls)* My father was a Law-Court
painter. I inherited all his connections, all his brushes, and
all his habits.

K

Well, what do you advise?

TITORELLI

That depends on the kind of acquittal you want. There are three kinds: there's real acquittal, there's apparent acquittal, and there's indefinite postponement.

K

Ah! . . .

TITORELLI

Real acquittal, pure and simple, is certainly the best; but I hasten to say I haven't the smallest influence in getting it. Nor has anyone, so far as I know. What's more, since I was a child, I've sat in on every great session of the Court. I've followed an infinite number of trials, and I must confess I've never come across a single case of real acquittal.

K

Did you ever hear of any that happened before your time?

TITORELLI

They say there have been a few. It's very hard to know exactly because the decisions of the Court are never published. The judges themselves don't have the right to see them, so that only legends exist about the Law of the past. Some of the legends, by the way, are very beautiful, and I've used some of them on occasion as subjects for my paintings.

K

But you can't cite these legends before the Court.

TITORELLI

No, you can't. That you certainly can't.

K

Then it's useless, I suppose, to talk about them. We'd better forget about real acquittal. You mentioned two other ways. . . .

TITORELLI

They're the only ones you can talk about. . . . But don't you want to take off your jacket before we start on them?

K

Gladly.
(He gets up.)
Couldn't we open the window?

TITORELLI

Impossible.

K

Not even for a few minutes?

TITORELLI

That's not a window. It's just a plate of glass in a frame.

K

(Reeling)
Awfully uncomfortable . . . and unhealthy, too.

TITORELLI

(Carried away)
Don't you believe it! The heat stays in much better this way than with double windows. Besides if I wanted to air the place, I'd just have to open one of the doors, or even both. But plenty of air comes in through the cracks in the walls.

K

I don't see another door.

TITORELLI

It's right behind you. Everything's so small here, I had to put the bed across the room.

K

Well, since you suggest it, I will. . . .
   (He takes off his jacket.)

THE LITTLE GIRLS

Oh! He's getting undressed!
   (They jostle each other to look through the cracks.)
Tito's going to paint his picture! . . .

K

What were the other two solutions called?

TITORELLI

Apparent acquittal and indefinite postponement. In either one of those, I can help you. But it's for you to decide which you want. Apparent acquittal demands a great effort, but a short one; indefinite postponement, a small chronic effort. We'll talk about the first one now, if that's the one you want.

K

   (Who is trying hard to follow)
Apparent acquittal?

TITORELLI

   (Continuing)
I'll write out for you, in the proper form, a certificate of your innocence. The wording of the certificate has been handed down to me by my father. It's beyond dispute. Then I'll take it to all the judges I know and have them sign it. I'll begin tonight with the Judge in the portrait I've just done, and

I'll swear to your innocence. I'll be committing *myself,* you see, so the Judge will have to believe me.

K

Believe you, yes. But will he acquit me?

TITORELLI

Just as I said. As soon as the certificate has enough signatures, the procedure is very rapid. Usually at this stage there are no more obstacles. It's about then too that the accused man feels most confident. He says good-bye to the Court. His case is over. And he's free.

K

(Starting)
He's free?

TITORELLI

Yes, but you understand, only apparently, or if you prefer, provisionally. You're forgetting that all the judges we're talking about are subordinate judges and don't have the right to grant a definite acquittal. It goes without saying that that's done only by the highest Court, which we can't reach, not you, not me, not anybody. Only a final acquittal destroys all the evidence of a trial, even the text of the acquittal itself. Nothing seen, nothing known; nothing remains.

K

And apparent acquittal?

TITORELLI

After that, nothing is thrown away, and the Law never forgets. The first accusation has lost none of its force, and any judge can pull it out, at any time.

K

And then?

TITORELLI

Well then there's a new arrest, naturally. The trial starts all
over again, and you have to pull all your forces together again
for a new apparent acquittal. You can't ever give up.

K

But tell me, isn't the second acquittal harder to get than the
first?

TITORELLI

No one could tell you very accurately about that.

K

And it isn't final anyway, is it?

TITORELLI

Of course not.
(Silence. He shakes his head.)
Apparent acquittal doesn't seem to satisfy you. It's possible
you would prefer indefinite postponement. Should I explain
what that's like?

K

If it isn't too much trouble.

TITORELLI

Well as the name suggests, it keeps your trial indefinitely in
its first stage. It requires constant contact with the Court.
But it offers one definite advantage over apparent acquittal—
it gives you a less uncertain future. The indefinite postponement guarantees you against the shock of a sudden new arrest.

(K throws his coat over his arm and gets up, ready to leave.)

THE LITTLE GIRLS

Oh, he's getting up! He's going to leave!

TITORELLI

What! Are you leaving already?

K

Yes! Yes!!

TITORELLI

The two methods have this in common—that they prevent the conviction of the defendant.

K

But they also prevent his real acquittal and freedom.

TITORELLI

You've grasped the point. I suggest you don't decide for either one right away. Their advantages and disadvantages balance each other. Weigh everything carefully; but don't forget that there isn't much time.

K

I'll come back soon.
(He goes to the door.)

TITORELLI

No. Go out the other way, so those little pests don't bother you.
(He points to the door behind the bed.)

THE LITTLE GIRLS

Hurry up! He's going out the other way.

TITORELLI

Just a moment. Wouldn't you like to buy one of my canvases?

K

I didn't presume to ask, but if it's all right. . . .

TITORELLI

(Showing a canvas)
This one is a heath.

K

(Hardly looking at it)
Fine. Perfect. I'll take it.

TITORELLI

And here's the one that goes with it. They enhance each other's value.

K

They're excellent landscapes. I'll take both of them for my office.

TITORELLI

If you like the subject so much. . . . Well, it's a lucky thing, because I have another one that goes with these.

K

(Who wants only to get out)
I'll take that one too. Give me the price of all three.

TITORELLI

We can discuss that later. I'm so pleased you like my pictures. I'll send you everything I have here. They're all paintings of heaths. Some people consider my landscapes too sad, but there are some like you who take to their melancholy.

K

(Impatiently)
All right, wrap them all up. I'll have a clerk pick them up tomorrow.

TITORELLI

That won't be necessary. I'll get a porter to take them along with you. . . . Just step over the mattress. You can't get out that door any other way. And when you're out, don't be alarmed to find yourself in the offices of the Court. My studio is part of them. The connection handicaps my work considerably, but there are compensations such as. . . . *(He calls the Bailiff.)* Casimir, take these canvases to Mr. K's office at his bank.

K

Before I leave, tell me one thing—who is Lanz the carpenter?
(The setting bursts open. The walls disappear and reveal a group of people, all bearded, standing in a semi-circle.)

TITORELLI

(Laughing)
Lanz the carpenter doesn't exist. It's a password.

In the downstage area, all the actors of the earlier scenes reappear. The setting is the same as in the scene with the Laundress. On the left is a little platform on which the Judge's table and chair are standing.

K

(Who doesn't believe his eyes)
What's this?

TITORELLI

(In the most matter-of-fact way)
This gentleman is asking about Carpenter Lanz.

*(General hubbub. Whispering by and near the Judge.
"Here he is."—"Yes, it's he."—"At last.")*

THE LAUNDRESS

*(Putting down her basket of laundry in a corner at stage
right)*
Yes, of course—we understand!

JUDGE

(In a loud voice)
Guards! No one else is to enter the courtroom.

K

(Ironically)
I see—a session behind closed doors.
*(He recognizes Mrs. Grubach and Miss Burstner, goes over
to shake hands with them.)*
Oh! Mrs. Grubach! How very nice!

MRS. GRUBACH

Why, Mr. K, it's only natural!

K

And Miss Burstner. . . . It was very nice of you to come.

MISS BURSTNER

I wouldn't miss it for the world! It's thrilling!
*(The Judge raps on his table. The conversations of the
spectators stop quickly. Silence.)*

JUDGE

Joseph K, we've been waiting for you for over an hour.
(In the courtroom, almost unanimous disapproval: "Boo!
Boo!")

LAUNDRESS

(Aside, to the spectators near her)
He always says that.

K

How could I know that. I hadn't been. . . .

JUDGE

(Interrupting)
That doesn't matter to us. The fact remains you're over an
hour late.
(Renewed murmurs of disapproval from the crowd)

K

(Almost arrogantly.)
Late or not, I'm here.
(Laughter and some applause from the crowd: "Bravo!
Bravo!")

JUDGE

Yes, but now we're under no obligation to hear you.
*(Murmurs of disappointment and blunt disapproval. The
Judge signals to everyone for silence.)*

ALL

Sh! Sh!

JUDGE

But we'll make an exception in your case, and hear you
anyhow.

*("Ah!" from all. The Judge begins to examine his dossiers
and getting lost in them, he adds:)*

Just a minute. Now we're the ones who aren't ready.

*(Disappointment. Everyone starts to leave in confusion.
The Judge jumps to his feet.)*

No one is to leave.

*(They all return docilely to their places. But a new disturb-
ance comes from the left wings. Some officials come in,
shouting:)*

OFFICIALS

Let us through! Let us through! Make way! Make way! The
Advocate! Let us through!

*(The Advocate's party appears: Leni, the Chief Clerk of
the Court, the Advocate on his bed, wheeled as in a baby
carriage by servants, and Block following them like a dog.)*

K

(Seeing the Advocate)

Oh no, for heaven's sake! Not him! I don't want him here,
for anything.

*(He zigzags through the crowd which is pushing and
shoving back to make way for the Advocate's entourage.)*

I've told you already I want to break with you.

(At this, astonishment. Everybody says, "You want to . . .")

K

(Continuing his cross)

Yes, break with you.

(He has come up to Leni, who takes his arm.)

LENI

Not with me, Joseph!

K

(Escaping from her)

With him. I've had enough, enough!

(Block, who had been standing motionless, maddened by this decision, now races about hysterically, swinging his arms, and exclaims:)

BLOCK

That's how he thanks his Advocate! That's how he thanks his Advocate!

ADVOCATE

Silence, Block!

(All movement stops. The crowd groups around them. Block goes to the foot of the Advocate's bed and squats.)

ADVOCATE

(To K)

I think that what brought you to this mistake is that up to now you've been shown too much consideration. If you knew the way the others are usually treated, it would be a valuable lesson to you. Is Block here?

BLOCK

At your service.

ADVOCATE

You've come at a bad time.

BLOCK

Didn't you call me?

ADVOCATE

Perhaps I did. But that doesn't prevent you from coming at the worst time. You always come at the worst time.

BLOCK

Do you want me to go?

ADVOCATE

Since you're here, you can stay. Who is your Advocate?

BLOCK

You know very well, my Advocate, that you are.

ADVOCATE

And besides me?

BLOCK

No one, my Advocate.

ADVOCATE

Then don't obey anyone but me.

BLOCK

I kneel to you, my Advocate.

K

(Angrily)

Fine. Crawl to him. Squat on all fours. Grovel in the mud.

BLOCK

(Furious, straightening up)

You, you have no right to speak to me like that. You especially, with your trial in its very first stages, you're not above
me in any way. You're accused too, you too. And you're wrong
if you think you're better than I am just because you're
standing up while I squat on all fours, as you say.

*(In a frenzy, he prostrates himself again and covers the
Advocate's hand with kisses.)*

My dear Advocate, listen how he speaks to me! Listen to him!
The time that his trial has gone on is still measured in days
and hours, and he insults *me* whose trial has been going on
for over five years.

K

Mr. Advocate, I am sufficiently enlightened by this scene. I
refuse your help and wish to conduct my trial alone.
(*Murmuring among the spectators. Then a heavy gong is
sounded.*)

ADVOCATE

Ah, it's foolish to anticipate it. It always comes as a surprise.

*The scene grows larger. The arches go up and reveal a
painted curtain representing a symphony of red robes.
Rows of pillars as in 17th century ceilings, drawing the
eye across the vista toward a stretch of blue sky.*

THE ATTENDANTS

Gentlemen, the Court.
(*More Judges come in.*)

ADVOCATE

(*Overcome*)
Leni! Leni! Come here to me, my child.

BLOCK

At last!

K

This isn't your trial; it's mine.

BLOCK

And I've been waiting for five years!

K

In the hole! In the hole!
(Wrestling with Block)

DEPUTY DIRECTOR

A little control, Mr. Manager. Good heavens, how you forget yourself.

UNCLE

Come, Joseph, take it easy, take it easy. Think of your family.
(During all this, the Judge has been consulting his ledger.)

JUDGE

Joseph K. . . .

K

Here, your Honor.

JUDGE

Step forward. You are a house-painter.

K

Excuse me, your Honor. It's just as I thought—there's been a mistake. I'm the Manager of an important bank.
(Laughter among the spectators.)

JUDGE

That makes no difference. Silence! . . . In that case though, I'll need a minute or two.
(Again he leafs through his ledger.)

LENI

Oh! How good-looking he is!

ADVOCATE

(To Titorelli)

It's an oddity of hers. She falls in love with all the accused. Nearly all of them seem beautiful to her; even Block. At least, at first.

TITORELLI

Lots of women get that feeling about them. And they're not making it up. It's a fact that being arrested brings about a noticeable change in the look of a man. As a painter I can recognize one of them right off, even in a crowd.

JUDGE

Accused, you may speak.

K

You asked me, to start with, your Honor, if I was a house-painter; or to be more accurate, you didn't ask me at all—you told me. A plain lie spoken like the simple truth. Now that's typical of the way this whole trial has been run against me. Now tell me—why did you choose me? I'm curious to know. Maybe if you rummaged carefully through that mess on your desk, if you leafed through that repulsive ledger you use instead of a mind and a human heart, crammed full of everybody's entrails—what a loathsome thing it must be to touch! *(The crowd is scandalized.)* I have no doubt you'd find my name inscribed in the good book. But by whom? And why? Can you tell me? Of course not. You don't know any more than I do—you simply obey orders. And if you found a name which happens to be mine, we both know—don't we?—that it could just as well be somebody else's too —a house-painter's for example—*(Laughter.)* who's just as innocent as I am. A name like . . . Well, not just anyone! It wouldn't be yours, would it, gentlemen? No, it wouldn't be yours. You were too smart to be caught with the accused.

125

You joined up with the accusers.

All right, then, I'm arrested. I can't prove my innocence since I don't know what I'm supposed to be guilty of, and I'm considered guilty if I don't prove my innocence. You see, then, what your justice adds up to: there's no way out. Distinguished proponents of the Law, I'm aware that I'm a small matter. But my case isn't an isolated one, and I'm not speaking for myself alone. I'm reminding you of all the innocent men who have been accused as I've been, and face the justice I face.

THE CROWD

Bravo! Bravo!

JUDGE

Silence in the Court! Give the accused his chance to speak.

K

Oh, I'm not trying to win prizes as an orator. All the legal gentlemen here, the little Judges and the littler Judges, the Magistrates and the Advocates, I'm sure they're much better orators than I am. It's their business. We, the accused, don't always know how to defend ourselves very well. And then our professional reputations aren't at stake. All we're defending is our freedom and our life. The Examining Magistrate just made a secret sign to somebody in the Court! Don't go to all that trouble, your Honor, spare your ingenuity. All you have to do is sing out your orders. Everybody here, I imagine, gets his orders from you. And somebody a little higher up gives you yours. I can feel it—behind my arrest, behind everything in this lunatic Court of Law—the grinding and turning of a whole machine with all of you trapped inside. All of you! The corrupt Inspectors and the stupid Guards and the mousy Attendants and the Judges in the biggest thrones whom we'll never speak to and can't even hope to see.

JUDGE

I should like to point out to you that in this preliminary session you are throwing away with your own hand the opportunity an interrogation invariably offers to the accused.

K

You can take your interrogation, you gang of criminals . . . If anybody touches me I'll knock him down!
(The bearded men present, at this exact moment, all raise their collars and reveal a very visible emblem: a big staring eye.)
Ah, I see! It's true. All of you are part of it; betrayers and slaves. The evil collected to watch the lowly, to mock me and deceive me. When you all applauded together, it was in the hope of making a fool of an innocent man. Don't try! I won't give you that satisfaction . . . What now? . . . You're silent now. Well, who are you then? What are you doing here? What does this mockery of Justice mean?
(All of them slowly turn away.)
How can it be, how can it be that you're human! You'll be going out of here, each one of you, back to your home, and kiss your mother and your wife and children . . . Each one of you all alone has a life—maybe even a conscience—you're bothered when you make a mistake, and you even like to say you're sorry. It's impossible to understand! And here, each one of you is lost in a solid bloc. You each hold up and hang on to and pull back the other. Each of you belongs to all, and even though none of you is under arrest, I feel, I know, you're less free than I am. Is it true or not, what I'm saying? Answer me! No, you don't want to, you can't, you don't dare answer me. Isn't there one man left, not one

honest man, among you? You're silent. Now all you want
to do is get out, go away . . . backwards . . . like this Justice
of yours . . . back into the dark . . . and leave me too in
the dark.

*(It is most important not to interrupt K's speech with too
much intermittent action. The crowd turns away and little
by little retreats out of sight, backwards. They disappear
through the passage-way in back and by way of the wings
on stage left and right.*

*The spectators: the Uncle, Miss Burstner, Mrs. Grubach,
Titorelli, etc., have retreated to the raised platform on
the left.*

*At this moment, the Deputy Director appears, cuts
stealthily into the solitude that surrounds K, and goes
into a huddle with him.)*

DEPUTY DIRECTOR

(Confidentially and very quickly)

Mr. Assessor, it looks as though you're no longer in complete
possession of yourself. Considering your condition, I thought
you'd like me to take over the confidential assignment they
wanted to give you.

K

(As if coming out of a dream)

What?

DEPUTY DIRECTOR

It's to show the city's art treasures and monuments to an
Italian client who's very important to the bank. He's on a
visit here for the first time. They remembered you were once
a member of the Society for the Preservation of Ancient
Monuments, but I told them you were very busy here. I'm
on my way to the cathedral, where the man is waiting for

you. I brought along a sightseer's guidebook to help me.
(The Deputy Director starts to go. K stops him.)

K

You've been aching, Mr. Director, aching to take over my job in every way. But this time you're not getting away with it.
(He snatches the album from his hands.)
I'm the one who's going to the cathedral.
(The Uncle, Miss Burstner and Titorelli, on the left, have watched the scene from the top of the platform.)

UNCLE

Joseph, don't be foolish . . . your trial. . .

K

It won't go any worse than when I take care of it myself.
(Wearily)
And then, I need to get away for a while.
(K puts on black gloves and goes out on the first level to the right.
The Deputy Director joins the three others on the platform and shrugs.)

MISS BURSTNER

What? He's leaving? . . .

TITORELLI

(Indifferent)
It's all right. They'll get along faster without him.
(A noise rises, drowns out everything, while the light deepens into night.)

END OF SCENE THREE

129

SCENE FOUR

At the Cathedral.
Change of scene. Cathedral columns. The pulpit, small,
in the shape of a shell; a little light, like a flickering flame,
undulates through the semi-darkness of the cathedral. It
is from a lamp the Chaplain is carrying. He, still quite
young, clean-shaven, with drawn face resembling Lacor-
daire's, climbs up to the pulpit and puts the lamp down
beside him. An effect of violet light from the stained glass
window completes the illusion of the Cathedral.

CHAPLAIN

The text for our sermon tonight is from the third chapter
of the Lamentations of Jeremiah. "Thou hast shut me in by
a wall, and no way can I escape. . . ."
(Pause)
My brethren, we must realize that these words of the prophet,
words of despair, are followed at once by words of comfort.
We will meditate on these together: "The Lord does not
cast off forever. . . ." Of course, the prophet adds. . . .
(The Chaplain stops and looks about him. Silence. And
in an entirely different tone, as if to himself:)
There's no one listening. *Vox clamantis in deserto.*
(K, almost invisible in the darkness, has come almost to
the foot of the pulpit.)

130

K

Father, I am listening, and I am in great anguish.

CHAPLAIN

Is it you, Joseph K?

K

Yes.

CHAPLAIN

Your trial is under way.

K

Yes.

CHAPLAIN

I've been looking for you. I am the prison chaplain and I had you come here to talk to you.

K

I didn't know that. I came here to show the cathedral to. . . .

CHAPLAIN

Details are not important. What are you holding in your hand? Is it a prayer-book?

K

It's a guidebook for sightseers.

CHAPLAIN

Put it down.
    (The guidebook falls to the floor.)
Do you know that your trial is going badly?

K

I suppose it is. I've worked very hard at it, but so far I've had no success.

CHAPLAIN

How do you think it will end?

K

Do you know?

CHAPLAIN

No, but I suspect it will end badly. They think you're guilty. They consider your crime is already proved.

K

I'm not guilty. Unless everyone is guilty. The Court is guilty of an error.

CHAPLAIN

It pains me to hear you utter such harsh words. You speak them out of pride. Instead of admitting your crime, you choose to turn against the Court the accusation which in your heart of hearts you know that you yourself have earned. But you're only adding to your original sin a sin that is even greater. You're pretending to be innocent, and accuse the accuser to exonerate yourself. This is what Almighty God meant when he said to Job: Dost thou condemn me that thou mightst be justified?

K

But what is my guilt? Where, in what did I sin?

CHAPLAIN

If you seek, you shall find. You want proof of your crime.

Isn't it in your punishment? You must recognize your error,
convince yourself of it: They have chastened me, therefore
I am guilty.

K

Are you, too, prejudiced against me?

CHAPLAIN

I have no prejudice against you.

K

Then why don't you come down from your pulpit? There
isn't any sermon to be given. No one is here. Come down
to me.

CHAPLAIN

Yes, now I can come down.
   (*He comes down from his pulpit holding his lamp in his
   hand, and approaches K.*)
I had to talk to you from up there at first. Otherwise I might
have been too easily swayed by sympathy, and would tend to
forget my duty, and the severity of my office. After all, I too
serve the Law.

K

Tell me, what *is* the Law you serve?

CHAPLAIN

I cannot answer that.
   (*They continue their conversation, walking slowly.*)
Now you tell me, what do you intend to do now?

K

Go on looking for help, wherever it might be. I don't know
where.

CHAPLAIN

You've gone on too long looking for the help of others.
(He holds out the lamp to K, who takes it.)

K

I have more confidence in you than in anyone else.

CHAPLAIN

Aren't you deluding yourself?

K

About what?

CHAPLAIN

About the Law. Do you understand who I am?

K

You're the prison chaplain, you told me so.

CHAPLAIN

And in that capacity, I serve the Law. I'm on duty as a sentinel. They've put me in charge of a single doorway to prevent anyone from passing through. But it's for you that I've been waiting. The door that I've been guarding, you see, was made for you alone.

K

But can you tell me nothing to relieve my anxiety?

CHAPLAIN

It is in your anxiety that you must find assurance. You must say to yourself, I am hunted, and so I am chosen.

K

But if I could only cry out my innocence. . . .

CHAPLAIN

The voice of the mute cries out in silence. The blind see in it, the deaf hear, solitude is crowded, darkness is filled with light. And what bows you to the ground, exalts you.

(The lamp K is holding goes out.)

Now I must leave you. My duties call me elsewhere. As for you, you are expected.

K

(An anguished cry)

Don't leave me! I can't find my way out alone in this darkness.

(The Chaplain goes off rapidly, and, in the distance, he says:)

CHAPLAIN

Go back to the wall on the left. Follow it closely and you'll come to a way out.

The light changes, becoming clear and blue: the light of dawn. The cathedral scene disappears and the platform in the rear is again visible. K, who followed along the wall on the right, approaches the center of the stage, readjusts his black gloves. He seems to have come from far off.

Two prison guards appear coming from downstage left and right. They are very tall and wear silk hats and frock coats. One of them is carrying a long butcher's knife in his belt. They advance toward one another and salute each other ceremoniously. They see K, who stands back; making a sign to each other, they go to him.

Workers, with their tool-kits, pass by rapidly on the platform, indifferent to what is going on. Some revelers and loose women in evening clothes: a Baudelaire-like dawn. From downstage right comes the Inspector, very dignified

*and impassive. He rolls a cigarette. The two prison guards,
on either side of K, greet the Inspector with elaborate
decorum.*

INSPECTOR

Gentlemen, you have your orders.
*(The hands of the prison guards clasp K's shoulders. They
do not speak. Their gestures alone must express, in the
face of K's astonished—and at first somewhat resistant—
reaction, that they do nothing but obey orders to which K
himself must submit.)*

K

If my poor Uncle were to see this, he would be horribly
upset. He's always taken so much trouble about the family.

INSPECTOR

(Gravely, as if to himself)
There's not much one man can do for another.

K

It's not so much for myself, but as a matter of principle. . . .

INSPECTOR

(Haughty, disdainful)
Don't worry about principles. There are others here to take
care of them.

K

If at least. . . .

INSPECTOR

What do you want to say?

K

(Hesitates a little, and then:)
Nothing.

(The Inspector shrugs his shoulders and goes off smoking his cigarette. The Guards grab K under the arms. He offers no further resistance. In fact he helps them and tries to make the job of the executioners easier.

The scene of the execution, according to preference, may be acted out upstage and somewhat concealed, or it may be done very plainly and realistically in the center of the stage [as in the plucking out of Gloucester's eyes in King Lear.] *In either case, it is to be performed in the spirit of a ritual.*

The Guards hesitate, each offering politely to let the other administer the final blow. One passes the knife to the other. K of his own free will has placed his head on the block—a simple paving-stone which the executioners have found lying on the ground, and have moved into place—and he assumes his position for execution. The Guards approve.

At this moment, in the background, the window of a far-off house lights up. K lifts his head and stretches out his hands: Is it a signal? The announcement of unlooked-for help? But the light goes out, and K's arms, with the useless gesture of a drowning man, fall back.

One of the executioners plunges the knife into K's heart. On the platform, a gentleman and his wife pass by. The lady stops for a moment, looking at the execution.)

LADY

Look! What are they going to do to him? It's very strange.

138

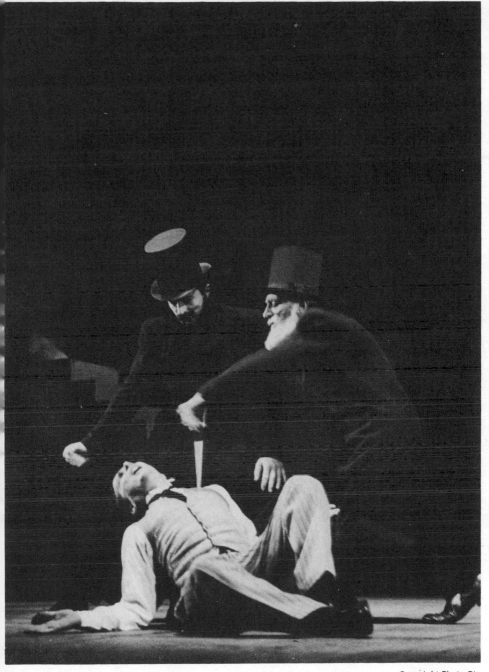

GENTLEMAN

(Who understands)

Come, my dear. These are matters of the Law. They have
nothing to do with us.

K

Like a dog!

CURTAIN